We Choose to Thrive

Our Voices Rising in Unison to Share a Message of Hope,
And Inspiration for Abuse Survivors.

Book 2 of Series
Compiled by Becky Norwood

We Choose to Thrive

Our Voices Rising in Unison to Share a Message of Hope,
And Inspiration for Abuse Survivors.

Book 2 of Series
Compiled by Becky Norwood

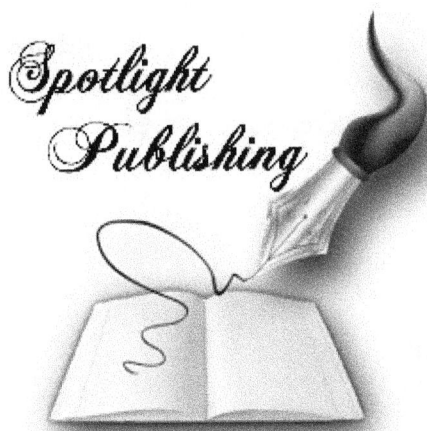

Spotlight Publishing

www.TheWomanILove.com
#WeChooseToThrive

Other Books by Becky Norwood

The Woman I Love: Surviving, Healing, and Thriving After a Childhood of Sexual, Emotional, and Physical Abuse. – Published August 2016
https://amzn.to/2IUPJjq

The Woman I Love: Journal and Coloring Book
https://amzn.to/2IRbfFG

We Choose to Thrive: Our Voices Rise in Unison to Share with Abuse Survivors a Message of Hope and Inspiration – Book 1 in Series
https://amzn.to/2GXgsPO

Women Innovators: Leaders, Makers, and Givers:
Women Who Make a Daily Difference
https://amzn.to/2JKlnl1

"Every great story on the planet happened when someone decided not to give up, but kept going no matter what.

Spryte Loriano

Table of Contents

We Choose to Thrive

Introduction

*A*s I contemplated yet another book in this series of We Choose to Thrive, I had to sit back and examine my motives and reassess the time and effort involved in bringing yet another book to our readers.

Let's face it. Putting together an anthology book of this nature is a lot of work. Getting the contributors to meet deadlines, submit their bio's and head shots, editing the videos we did for each, and coordinating all the details takes time, effort and cooperation from all of the participants.

So why do I do it? Heaven knows I have a lot on my plate already, with the busyness of being a business owner and the responsibility of helping raise three grandchildren and helping their mama wade her way through divorce and single parenthood.

It is because of each of you, the co-authors in this book and our previous book, the first in this series. Having walked this road of overcoming deeply scaring abuse, I know firsthand the courage it takes to rise above the pain, to begin the healing journey and the decision it takes to follow it through.

For far too long, I kept looking back into that rear-view mirror, with the woulda, coulda, shoulda, and a plethora of other issues, which were based entirely on shame, guilt, and fear. When I first stood and shared my story out loud, and subsequently wrote my story and published it, my life changed drastically for the better. Once I released it out to the world, the pain was set free!

And then came the first in the series of We Choose to Thrive and the thirty women who chose to participate. I witnessed women sharing their stories, often for the first time. I listened to their stories as we created their videos to accompany the book. And better yet, I watched in wonder and awe as I saw the transformation that occurred for them too.

So, it is with deep respect, awe, and joy, that I acknowledge each of you that have courageously chosen to participate in this second book of the series, as well as the first.

You come from varied backgrounds and different kinds of abuse. You have experienced the gut-wrenching pain, and the long road to recovery, and yet you did not give up! And for that, I honor you with deep respect.

If you are reading this book, we each sincerely hope that even one story will catch your heart and inspire you to decide once and for all that YOU CHOOSE TO THRIVE as well.

Let's face it, abuse is abuse, no matter what kind of abuse it is, and it cuts deep. As more of us stand up and speak out, perhaps we can change the world that comes behind us. By sharing our stories and uniting as a sisterhood who says "NO MORE!," the awareness sinks in deeper, and we find ample support to know that we are not alone.

In my own healing journey, I have done a lot of reading, attended many events that discussed the power of our minds and positive thinking. One piece of work that gave me pause for reflection was the work by Dr. David Hawkins.

In a nutshell, his teaching is that everything in our world, indeed, throughout the universe is vibrating energy. While I will not pretend to claim to understand how he measures the energetic scale of emotions, let alone everything else, like water, for instance, I resonated with what he says based on how I feel when I am happy versus how I feel when I am sad or depressed. You will see the scale, (Dr. David Hawkins' image is shaped like a pyramid.) I kept the scale but have used the image of a woman with arms raised in up in triumph over the fact that she had risen from the shame, guilt, grief, and fear, found the courage (the most difficult part) and rose up to acceptance, love, joy, peace and beyond.

It is a fascinating study, but what I wanted to get across to our readers is that there is a transformation that occurs when we decide to share our stories. In my experience, as I began putting pen to paper to write the words, thoughts, and memories that came flooding back, and yet the writing of the words made the sadness of those memories lose their power. It set me free, and this is how many of the women who have shared their stories feel.

We live in amazing times, where the #me too movement has many coming forth. Ultimately, I hope that it will produce a kinder, gentler society with much more respect and love for others.

At any rate, it is creating awareness, and with that awareness, maybe a there will be a better world.

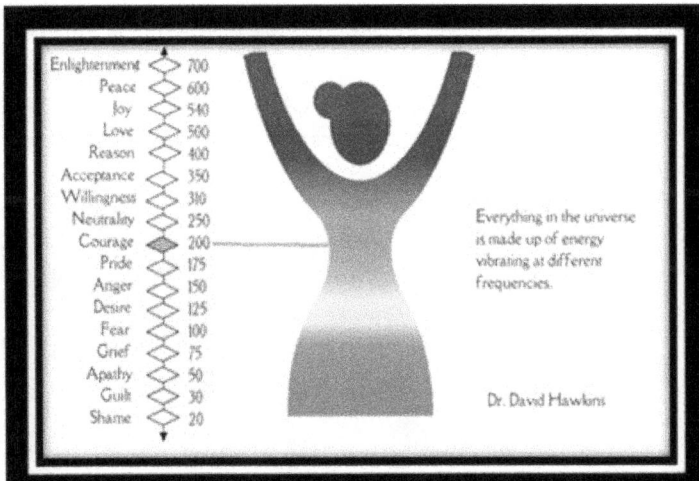

http://www.mindvalley.com/christie-marie-sheldon/love-or-above/?OrderID=&msk=
https://www.healerslibrary.com/news/dr-david-hawkins-scale-consciousness-emotion-code/

We Choose to Thrive

Acknowledgments

*I*t has been fascinating, how, when sharing my book, and this project, in conversations with women, the stories that begin to unfold. From those stories, friendships and sisterhood have formed not only in my relationships but, for those who have participated in this project and the many others much like this one that is taking place.

There is Oshikan Sjodin-Bunse, who wrote not only the foreword for this book but also a chapter. We met at an event where I had a display table. She'd traveled from Germany to attend this event, and it was at that event that not only did we enjoy a delightful dinner together, as we shared stories and visions for the work we are both doing, but she also became the perfect fit for contributing the foreword. On a subsequent trip to the U.S., she took time out of her travels to stop for a visit and preparation for this book.

Then there is Lise Lavigne, whom I met in Canada. Once again, a connection that turned into a friendship as we shared with each other not only our stories but also our passion to be the change in this world. She is now a leader in our private Facebook group, a safe place for healing and support to take place. https://www.facebook.com/thewomanilove

I applaud Johanna Alperin whose poem graces the first chapter of this book. Her story is so gut-wrenching, and she is so fresh out of the devastation of unbelievable cyber-attacks that we could not safely share her story in the pages of this book. Her efforts to heal, find normalcy and feel safe in our world shows a spirit that shines brightly.

There is Brenda Hammon with Sacred Hearts Rising, do much the same as we are doing here, and whose book I likewise participated in.

To the feisty and fiery Jane M. Powers, who is a force to be reckoned with as she encourages others to find their voice and be heard.

To the amazing, insightful and true friend, Sue Ferreira, who was the one who first challenged me to share my story, after listening to me rant as we walked the beautiful coastline of La Jolla, CA.

To Natalie McQueen, whose passion for finding ways to support those most in need of support. Your heart is huge, your smile and wisdom amazing and most of all your friendship is treasured as we figure how to combine our experiences into an amazing business. Juliana Riviera shared her story in this book at Natalie's encouragement.

To Shannon O'Leary, who hails from Australia, whose story graced our first book in this series, and who wrote her book sharing her story. Shannon returned to share an incredible story about Grace, a 90+-year-old woman who told her story to Shannon. She had never told a soul. I shudder to think of those who have gone to the grave having carried the pain and devastation of abuse in silence!

To Diana Dunham Young, who regularly stays in touch with me and sends fitting and powerful quotes as a reminder and encouragement to stay the course.

I wish I could go on an on and give all the praise that is due to the many I wish to tell you about. But the one who gets the most praise in my heart is my amazing, loyal, loving and kind husband, Mark. Honey, I love you, and thank you for always being the wind beneath my wings.

Foreword

By Oshikan Sjodin-Bunse

$\mathcal{B}$ecky Norwood had foresight. Before the #MeToo Movement brought widespread awareness to workplace assault and harassment, and the #TimesUp Movement began giving practical help to those not privileged enough to take legal recourse without support, Becky was writing about her abuse experience. She understood the healing power of sharing one's own story; of the benefit for oneself and for other survivors, even with all the costs that may accompany doing so.

Becky wrote a book about her recovery from the after-effects of the abuse she experienced from her father, titled, 'The Woman I Love'. She then encouraged fifty women to write their stories of how they are now thriving after abuse! The book you are holding in your hands is book two in the series, 'We Choose to Thrive'.

Victims of abuse are joining together and speaking out to counteract oppressive silence, feelings of shame and the resulting free pass that allows abusers to continue their insidious behavior. We have become a force that is bringing, hopefully, great winds of change.

The #MeToo Movement concentrates on workplace abuse. The individual stories here encompass physical, sexual, emotional and psychological abuse, perpetrated by all kinds of people in all kinds of places. Detailing extreme scenarios of the lowest of behaviors that human beings are capable of is not the point of our stories. We have included some detail to add clarity and to shine a light on the various ways that abuse stays clandestine, often in ones' very own home.

Our stories speak of how each of us are thriving in our own way and how we got there. But what does it really mean to thrive after abuse? Our answers are individual and varied but with a red thread weaved throughout all of our stories. We feel much freer, happier and successful!

"People change for two main reasons; either their minds have been opened or their hearts have been broken." ~ Steve Aitchison.

The author's hearts were broken and our minds were opened. As we heal our minds and hearts we encourage you to do so too.

Learning and evolving is a life-long adventure if we choose to foster self-growth. Our transformational journey does not end until we do, and it certainly can become a lot more light-filled and fun! We authors been through a lot and have taken responsibility to learn how to be respectful and loving with ourselves and stay away from abusers. We are now passionate to contribute in whatever way we can to the awakening on how to live as thriver's after abuse.

We understand that being the target of abuse was not our fault. We know that we didn't deserve it, even if we were indoctrinated to believe that we did. We did not want it and yet it happened. And still, we came out on the other side! We have moved on, or are in the process of moving past the internalized and raw pain.

Maybe you have experienced 'power over', bullying, degrading and harmful behavior targeted at you? It is our hope that if you are still caught in the claws of any kind of abuse, you will gain strength from our stories, reach out to us and make use of our gathered knowledge and experience with different healing methods. You can practice kinder ways of seeing yourself that we model for you. We support you in extracting yourself from an abusive situation. It is certainly not always an easy or simple thing to do, but know that you are not alone! Please draw from the strength and resilience that you find among these pages. We stand with you in solidarity!

For many the risk of speaking up at this time is too severe. But you can read books! You can get curious about what you can do to act on your recovery. You can educate yourself about toxic people and the effects their behavior has on you. You can prepare to leave. You can learn to set boundaries and remove the abuser from your life.

In less severe and fortunate situations, you may be able to encourage the abuser to get help, but please do not make this your priority. Much precious time can be wasted, as many have no intention of changing. You can attract positive and supportive people into your life. You can and must protect your children, which means also protecting yourself. You can stop believing that all of this is just too hard. You can remember who you are and give yourself the love and respect that is your birthright! Let your curiosity and amazing resilience, which you may not even know you possess yet, be your guide.

You don't have to spend any more time suppressing, ruminating, acting out, feeling ashamed, or sabotaging yourself once you get curious and act on your recovery. Transforming the hopeless, helpless, fearful, rage and grief-filled emotions that accompany an abuse survivor, feels wonderful! It opens you to new possibilities within yourself!

Once you find ways to gain a sense of peace about your abuse experience, then you have the zest in your head, heart and hands to concentrate on other things. You have freedom to put energy into what you really love to do, what calls to you and how you can bring beauty into this world. You are wiser. You might even use your experience, plus training, to help others recover from the after-effects of abuse, as some of us have made into our life work.

In book two, you can feel the passion of the twenty authors as they share tried and true helpful mindsets and healing methods. We are like encyclopedias of various practices that can help victims of abuse recover.

You just have to pick what resonates with you and where you are on your healing journey. Then learn how to do and practice! Without the various steps of recovery being spelled out in every chapter, you will vicariously be traveling on many a healing journey as we step from victim to survivor to thriver.

The women in this book, who have done so much to heal from the bad behavior and abusive neglect inflicted upon them, are not going to be passing on an abusive legacy to their own children or children in their care. More children are less likely to need to recover from abuse or copy bullying behavior because their parent, teacher, spiritual guide or sports coach broke the ugly chain of abusive behavior that is too often passed down from old to young. We also are not the ones who partake in horrible patterns of hurtful behavior towards other adults. We know what it means as thriver's to practice loving kindness and respect, both for ourselves and with others.

"Walk your path without fear, regardless of others attitudes. Be who you were born to be." ~ Anonymous

Messages from Past Participants

"I had never shared my story with anyone who put it down on paper. In telling my story. Becky Norwood made me feel safe and loved and I hope in some small way my courage to tell my story will encourage other survivors to do the same."

-Diana Dunham

"My name is Shanna Maria, I was one of the 31 women featured in Becky Norwood book series We Choose To Thrive.

Being a part of this book was a powerful, incredibly freeing & empowering experience. There is magic that happens when we come together and share. I am honored and grateful to have been a part of this experience.

Becky Norwood is amazing to work with as she is with you throughout this journey and made it simple not overwhelming she is truly an earth angel and one I am proud to call friend.

Why I choose to be in this book was because I saw the vision of what this book meant for not only myself but for others to see that you can thrive after abuse it's not my identity it's something that happened. She gave us a platform to not only survive but to thrive.

This book is packed full of powerful stories of how each one of us triumph over the challenges to thrive in life. This book show cases how each one of us were able to stand up, speak up, Empower and conquer. There is light at the end of the tunnel!"

Love & Light, Shanna Maria
www.facebook.com/ShannaMaria2016
Instagram: @shanna_maria_201

"There is no greater way to heal than to find your voice. Breaking the silence and speaking your truth is powerful and freeing. We Chose to Thrive gave me a means to share my story and support others in doing the same. I encourage you to do the same!"

Jane M Powers -"Let's Talk Impact"-www.janempowers.com

"Opening the gateway for growth, self-discovery, a bond of sisterhood and a connection to incredible women that will never fade…That is what being part of We Choose To Thrive, Our Voices Rise in Unison has created for me."

Teresa Syms - Lifeologist, Intuitive Life Coach
Author: A Century of Secrets
www.TeresaSyms.com

"In August 2016, I made contact with Mrs. Becky Norwood, after learning from the national organization, R.A.I.N.N, (Rape, Abuse, Incest, National Network), for which I was a Public Speaker, that Becky was looking for individuals who had been sexually abused as a child and was willing to share their story.

I connected immediately with Becky during our initial communications. We had so much in common. Both of us were authors, Becky being a best seller author for her novel titled, "The Woman I Love" and I authoring the novel, "Don't Run Away Make A Way Queen, acronym DRAMA Queen."

The common denominator in our novels was that we both encountered sexual abuse in our lives, we were brave enough to no longer empower our fears, and we were able to find our voices and journal our uncomfortable past. Becky's goal was to find several other prominent, powerful, successful, thriving women in society, who also was willing to not only speak about their abuse but to stand on their platform in life, reflecting all of their accomplishments in spite of their past adversities.

I did not have the opportunity to personally meet all of the other 30 women in the 1st, "We Choose To Thrive," but we do have a place that we can meet and have conversations with other persons, who are finding their voices and speaking out about their abuse, in a secured online chatroom.

I thank Becky for providing my "Choose To Thrive Family," a place where they can be safe and have a dialogue with others who can relate to their circumstances.

We would not be the productive, articulate, fascinating, caring persons that we are today, had we not stepped out on faith, put our fears behind us, by having a dialogue, being open and vulnerable to discuss our common thread, "Sexual Abuse."

Thank you to All of the persons who have contributed to the next series novel, "We Choose to Thrive." Wishing you all continued thrivorship, success, good health and looking forward to reading the novel, and meeting with you in the near future."

Mickey See-Asia aka Michele D. Croswell
Best Seller Amazon Author

"When I first inquired of your invitation, little did I know that my story would be part of such a story with a voice. You met me with feeling and held my views and heart as a precious jewel. Your work and your interviews will continue to change lives all over the world."

Edna J. White
Author: Stuff!: Giving Voice to the Secret of Childhood Sexual Abuse

"I loved each and every chapter of this wonderful book. The lives of each woman, and their strength through their stories are inspiring. Thank you Becky for gathering these 31 woman to share their lives, on how they not only survived but are living proof that you can Thrive."

Christina Wensell

"Working with Becky Norwood has been an incredible experience. I am honored to be included and share a part of my story in her new book, We Choose To Thrive. Becky has been so helpful, responsive, and caring - a joy to work with. I hope that my story helps others, as I know that Becky's story has helped me."

Nikki Dubose
Author: Washed Away from Darkness to Light

"Being part of the We Choose To Thrive project has been one of the most important things in my continued recovery from the horrible abuse I suffered. Being able to share in such a supportive environment with other courageous women doing the same has been a gift. Helping others heal from this abuse is what gives what happened to me purpose and meaning.

Thank you Becky Norwood and everyone else who is a part or had a part in making this project happen. We are warriors."

Janet Bentley

"An amazing book filled with stories of surviving trauma and going beyond surviving to thriving. A book filled strength and healing from women who have the courage to tell their stories and help others to heal. Becky Norwood is an amazing woman and I'm so glad she brought us together."

Terri Lanahan
Author: Hear My Voice: One Woman's Journey from Victim to Thriving After a Childhood of Abuse

"The best part of being involved in Book 1 of "We Choose to Thrive" is finding a sisterhood. Finding people that have shared similar circumstances and mindsets. Knowing that I shared my experiences with people who wouldn't judge, and more importantly would understand. Hearing and reading each other's stories helped me feel less ashamed and more empowered."

Roberta Brown
Author: The Shoulding-A Story of Resilience and Hope

"Many years ago, when I began creating and exhibiting art that expressed my stories of survival, gallery visitors expressed gratitude for my work as a tool for providing them the words for feelings they could not express. It became clear that sharing my own journey of recovery inspired others to persevere on their journey, and I felt compelled to continue.

Even though art continues to be the voice of my soul, and through my art making I have publically screamed in pain, and sang for joy, the idea of me being a public speaker still seems surreal! Yet, as I stepped off stage today, it struck me that I have been a professional member of the Canadian Association of Professional Speakers since 2008. You might not consider that an extraordinary achievement, but I know it is.

You see, growing up, I was a little girl silenced by an unwritten rule that was stated daily; "Little girls should be seen, but not heard," and trying to be a good little girl, I lived by this rule for far too long. I was raised in a home governed by fear and shrouded in secrecy. I had a lot to say, but I didn't feel that I could speak to anybody and say what really going on in my world. So I kept quiet, and as the silence deafened me, the voice of my soul screamed within.

Then I found art! Well, when I say I found "art," I should really say that I found "mark-making" as that was what I was doing. I started to doodle on scraps of paper and found relief, so I drew, scribbled, sculpted, and painted. The more I made marks, the more relief I felt. Indeed, I had found art-making as a way of being my voice, a sort of visual voice.

For me, being able to sketch my thoughts and feelings, scream out my fears, and ask for help, all came out in the doodles and scribbles using color and texture. They weren't beautiful pieces that wound be hung on the walls, but they were expressions of my inner voice. Not everyone could understand whay my art was saying, but I was empowered by each piece I created. I wasn't considered an artist, in fact, I failed art in high school because the school had a list of things I should draw, and none of them expressed how I felt, so I didn't draw them.

Thankfully, I applied for art school, and they recognized my expressive ability and deemed me "trainable," ignoring my failing grade. Art was primarily how I conversed with those around me until I gradually found myself delivering presentations on the healing power of art.

The more I was requested to share my experience from the stage with my art as the backdrop, the easier it became. To date over 70,000 people have seen my art and heard my message from the stage, and many more have been reached through the screen. Over time, this little girl silenced, has become a professional speaker, and now I return to the start as I am nearing the end of my training and will soon be a Professional Art Therapist.

So, I will you to try mark-making, discover art, and express your soul Grab a pencil, a crayon, and a scrap of paper, and just start making marks. You will be amazed at how your inside voice starts to come out, your soul will speak, and feel a little better, just because it has been heard. Art has a magical way of expressing beyond words, and in turn healing wounds.

May your heart heal through art!
Cheryl-Ann Webster

Warrior

Her smile had shattered,
And tears streamed no more.
She was broken fully,
Right down to the core.

She stirred, and she stirred, as the terror lurked with no end in sight.
Weak and alone it was time she admitted,
She had long lost her fight.

How could a girl who'd fought hopeless battles before,
Get to a place she'd lost everyone she had ever fought for?

Who was this shieldless warrior, not a soul had a clue;
A stranger to herself she pondered, 'what's the right thing to do?'

SHE WANTED TO QUIT,
SHE YEARNED TO FLEE; BUT…
SHE COULDN'T, WHY?
BECAUSE THAT WARRIOR WAS ME.

So broken and battered she rose as high as she could,
Even at half-mast, her mission could only do good.

Attack after attack,
She tried to help all.
Never an option,
Just this Warriors call!

The greater fight she wasn't equipped for;
She needed new ammo if she dares proceed more.

We Choose to Thrive!

The warrior in her had become such a force;
A few brave soldiers joined her, to seek out the source.

She warned them with great haste;
This mission was ugly, something no one should face.

But the few she'd sought out had talents unique;
They bravely entered the dangerous game hide-and-seek.

They hadn't the tools, nor did they know the route to take.
Only certain of the end goal, safety; for everyone's sake.

The force they were fighting was causing havoc galore;
This was no battle but a full-blown war.

What had she done, the warrior no one truly knew?
She often asked herself, as the suffering grew and grew.

Often she regretted letting anyone join in.
The pain was unbearable; it seemed they just couldn't win.

As her army fought on through unmarked terrain relentlessly,
The warrior often pondered, should there be a cost to be FREE?

SHE NEVER QUIT,
SHE DIDN'T FLEE; WHY?
BECAUSE, THAT WARRIOR IS ME!

By Johanna Alperin

Recording by Johanna
http://bit.ly/2JXB3RT

Magic Happens When We Inspire and Encourage Each Other

By Wendy Foster

The issues in my life began, as I believe most do, with early childhood trauma. I cannot recall the age my sexual abuse started, but I do know it was before I was able to walk. It was through much counseling and research regarding the body memories I experienced that I even discovered it at all.

I also suffered the sudden loss of my father to suicide when he violently took his own life in the basement of our family home. It was about six weeks before my 3rd birthday and about three months before Christmas. My whole family was devastated, but that kind of loss. Having happened at the tender age at which it occurred to me, it seems to have set me up for a whirlwind of issues that I would not discover, or recover from for decades.

Another terrifying incident happened on my first trip to the store by myself. I was mugged by two older boys who knocked me down, took the change purse, and ran. Almost as traumatizing as the event itself, was the ride in the back of a police car, which my Mom had flagged down after finding me distraught and disoriented (most likely in shock). We did find the boys, and one was sent to juvenile detention since this was not his first run-in with the law, but that was no consolation to me. In fact, it had the opposite effect. That experience haunted me for years. Due to my impressionable age at the time, I had great fears, including nightmares, that the "bad guy" would come back to get his revenge on my family and me. Due to these early childhood traumas, I learned some very clever and effective coping mechanisms. Be quiet. Be the good girl. Don't cause any problems. Keep the peace. In effect - be invisible. They served me well in my early years, and I became quite the pro as the years went on. I was not seen nor heard.

I became the mediator when there was conflict. I was the calm presence that could cool heated conversations, angry outbursts, and potential violence. I could lower the yelling and loud voices that scared the pants off me. I could sometimes prevent my younger siblings from getting "the belt" for their "bad behavior." I was a very powerful child of 8 - 10, now that I think of it.

I learned to parent at an early age, too. I took it upon myself to be the care-giver for my younger siblings - to keep them safe and have them avoid any of the experiences that I had endured. I think I did my job well, but it was not my job to do. The role of caregiver can take a toll on one as well, and in my teen years, it consumed me. I would far rather look after my siblings so Mom and Dad could go dance than go out with my friends to teen dances and social functions. I felt safer in that care-giving role at home.

All these magnificent coping mechanisms are wonderful when we are young. They keep us safe and give us some measure of control over our circumstances and our lives. They don't, however, serve us well as adults. These skills, which were so effective in my early years, would be the very things that I would later have to "unlearn" to be effective in leading a healthy, adult life.

Fast forward to my 40th year. I've just left my second marriage and discovered that much of our life was a lie. Our business was in huge debt. My husband had disappeared, actually leaving the country and not telling anyone about it. We had a 14-year-old daughter who was rebelling, grieving her losses, and handling her life circumstances as best she could. I was at the most confident time in my life, ready to start fresh and live the life of my dreams in my new career as an Empowerment Coach when my world came crashing down. Thank God I still had strength at that time, or I might not have survived what life would challenge me with next.

The pain was so great that, more often than I would like to admit, I numbed myself with alcohol. It was the only way I knew to give myself enough relief to force the measly four hours of sleep I could get before starting my next day. I was on a spiraling path, leading right to hell.

When my daughter left home to live with her friend's family, that was the last straw. I believed that I had failed as a wife and was now failing as a mother. I was failing at trying to keep the business afloat, and I had nothing left. It was December and with Christmas fast approaching, my spirits were anything but festive. I had reached my breaking point and decided the world would be a better place without me in it. I wrote a letter to my daughter apologizing for being such a failure and told her she would be much better off living with her friend's family. I then proceeded to take a large dose of pills, chasing it down with copious amounts of alcohol.

The Universe had other plans. My daughter and her friend's Mom came to the house and found me on the floor. They called for an ambulance, and I spent the most horrendous night in a cell-like, concrete room all alone with my pain and failed attempt at ending it.

I won't go into the nasty details of my time at the hospital. It is something I would wish on nobody. The point is, I did not get the help I needed.

I recently looked back at my hospital records, and it states that I suffered from far more than depression and alcohol abuse. I was suffering from something I have been articulating to my doctor for years.

But, that information would not be shared, and the help would not come for several years and several more trips to the ER. Little did I know that one of the downsides of my coping behavior would be self-sabotage. And, boy did I get good at that one.

I sabotaged two marriages. I severed key relationships. Most of all, I sabotaged my happiness, peace, and joy in life.

Finally, last year, after my second trip to the ER in 10 days, somebody took my cries for help seriously. And, lucky for me, I was unsuccessful in my third attempt to take my own life.

It is now a well known scientific fact that early childhood trauma is the main factor in almost every mental health issue. The research now available would have made my life much more bearable and my thoughts, behaviors, and actions much more understandable.

I had a consult in the hospital with a psychiatrist who listed off some of the traits of the condition, for me to consider. Tears immediately welled up in my eyes as I recognized myself in trait after trait, not believing this stranger could know me so well. What a relief! When he gave me a diagnosis of Borderline Personality Disorder, I was relieved that I was not alone and that I was not crazy after all-something I've joked about most of my life.

In the next moment, I realized that, with this diagnosis, comes a great burden, the burden of stigma. I had a choice to make at that moment-focus on the stigma and be filled with fear, or focus on the choices and be empowered.

I chose empowerment. From that moment, I committed to being the face of transformation for women's mental health, and I take that stand seriously. I am out to eradicate stigma and replace judgment, fear, blame, shame, and guilt with understanding, compassion, empathy, support, and love.

It was the most important thing I've done for myself in my healing journey. I am the voice for those who are unseen, unheard - for those who cannot or will not speak up for themselves. I gain my strength from inside myself with the help and support of my family, therapist, my research, and my continued work on being the best version of me that I can be. Creating awareness of the pain that underlies mental health issues, including the stigma, and misunderstanding is my way of helping others. I courageously and with vulnerability share my story so I can be the voice for those with no voice, or no choice.

I started out sharing my story with 60 powerful businesswomen at a leadership conference. That experience led to sharing with 1,200 participants at a women's run for mental health. And, from that presentation, I was the invited to be the keynote speaker to hundreds of affluent business people in Vancouver.

As I proceed on my journey of helping others, I continue to heal, expand, and grow myself. I am truly blessed to be on this path, and I embrace every experience that has led me to this place.

How could I possibly have taken on such a huge endeavor if I had not lived the life I have lived?

My words of wisdom for every woman who has a story to share regarding experiences that have affected her life are: Share them. First, know that you are not alone. Find a great coach or counselor to give you the tools, skills, and support you need. Next, create a circle of women who understand, support, and love you-who hear you, see you, and truly care. Be there for them as they are for you. Magic happens when we inspire and empower each other. Choose your support team carefully-especially your family members. Not everyone will give you the support you need. Put yourself and your healing journey first. Release the rest with love.

Educate yourself! Research, read, and devour information that supports you. Study brain science/neuroplasticity, etc. so you can see the scientific evidence of how we are affected by these early childhood traumas and more importantly, how we can and do overcome them.

At present, my two favorite resource books are: "In the Realm of Hungry Ghosts" by Dr. Gabor Mate, and "You Are Not Your Brain" by Dr. Jeffery Schwartz. There are also many videos on any topic that will inspire and empower you. Check out the above-listed authors as well as the amazing Ted Talks-offering a wealth of inspiration and education.

We Choose to Thrive!

Most of all, learn to love yourself. Love your past and embrace every bit of it. There are nuggets in there that will become gold to you; you'll simply have to dig for it. Take care of yourself and put yourself first. Be curious about who you are, your thoughts, behaviors, and actions. Be gentle with yourself as you learn new ways of living, coping, being.

And, most of all, keep being brilliant and live the life you were meant to live. Let your light shine and encourage others to do the same. Embrace the beauty and power that is uniquely YOU!

With healing love and hugs,
Wendy

Wendy Foster

Wendy Foster believes that women are the ones to be the change we want to see on the planet, creating the foundation for a loving, compassionate, and peaceful world.

Wendy has a dynamic personality, high voltage energy, and an extreme passion for teaching others. She is the intuitive catalyst for leaping out of comfort zones, busting through hidden blocks, and creating big, bold, delicious lives both personally and professionally.

Chief Empowerment Officer at GEM Consulting
Changing lives one heart at a time.
Phone: 778-533-1345
wendyfostercoach@gmail.com
www.gemconsulting.ca
https://www.facebook.com/wendy.foster.14606
Video Interview: https://youtu.be/GnUqWSU-pUA

"Be the light in the darkness to inspire and to enlighten others."

Debasish Mridha

Permission to Let Go

By Katie Hulbert

*M*y life story is multi-layered. When I was three years old, my parents joined a cult that was based on of the Shepherding Movement. For those who aren't familiar; it's comparable to "Jonestown, minus the Kool-Aid." (Wikipedia)

Quite frankly that description is pretty accurate. The movement was based on the concept of complete, authoritative control; i.e., you do whatever your shepherd, (AKA your pastor/leader) tells you to do, no questions asked. There was one person quoted, saying, "If God Almighty was standing in front of me and I knew it was him, and he told me to do something, and my shepherd told me to do something else, I would do whatever my shepherd said."

Suffice to say; there was a lot of overt mind control and manipulations as well as subtle brainwashing. In addition to the spiritual abuses, that type of environment was a breeding ground for extremely disturbed, perverse people. As a result, there was a large amount of sexual and physical abuse done in secret, behind closed doors, to which I was subjected along with many others. Not everyone in power participated in these abuses, but with the very perverse and twisted environment the movement provided, it was surprisingly easy for pedophiles and disturbed individuals to have massive amounts of unchecked power.

The second layer of abuse was my home life. It was very chaotic. My father has multiple personalities, (now termed "Dissociative Identity Disorder," instead of MPD). It didn't get diagnosed until later when I was 20 years of age, so growing up I didn't understand the "ins and outs" of what was happening. As a kid, it was just chaos, all the time. One minute somethings happening and the next something different. For example; I accidentally broke a window. He and I shared a hearty laugh, followed by his jovial words "Let's not tell your mom, ha ha ha ha." Fifteen minutes later, I'm being screamed at by him about the same thing as if the previous conversation didn't happen. (I now understand he didn't remember).

To give a clear picture: I was experiencing all this abuse going on at church and school which were one and the same). Then, we've got a bit of crazy-ville at home, which created this massive internal instability for me. I never knew where I stood, or what was coming next. It created this internal fight or flight 24/7 inside.

There was never any peace. It was just a constant state of fear. We lived in a communal environment; shared property, church, school, the whole deal. Imagine this; when I was away from home, it was scary, and a lot of horrible shit is happening, and then when I go home, it's also scary, and horrible shit was happening. The cherry on top was the third layer of abuse; the sexual abuse perpetrated upon me by family members early in my formative years. All of this added together made for a layered experience that consisted of pain, shame, and fear.

As I became an adult, my healing journey has taken quite some time and effort. At age 25, the depression, born of deep pain, self-hatred, and profound suppressed rage, began to take over. An emotional meltdown occurred when I was in my last year of college. I was driving to school, actively planning my suicide.

In the car, I had a profound experience that changed my life. The best words I have to describe it, which will never truly relay the magnitude of it, is this; I had a power encounter with God! I felt what I now describe as the physical presence of God. It was both dense and light, very scary and yet the most peaceful feeling I have ever felt. I heard an audible voice say,

"Go to the hospital, go to the hospital, go to the hospital."

I had never experienced anything quite like that, and it remains my most profound spiritual experience to date. I obeyed. I drove to the hospital, checked myself in at the psych ward, and said, "If you don't help me, I'm walking out of here, and I'm ending it." I got the help I needed that day, and it was the beginning of my healing journey.

The doctor put me on anti-depressants, and after about a week, it was like a light went on. It was like I got my sanity. The anti-depressants truly did help me physically. I think my emotional scale before Prozac was negative 10 to 0. The absence of anxiety was my best day!

Somebody else's zero (worst day) was my, "Whew, I'm functioning. Yeah!" (aka my best day).

The drugs put me back into the normal 0-10 scale. I still had emotion. It was just normal emotion, appropriate emotion. It stabilized me internally. I felt kind of normal for the first time, and it was at that time I thought, (and I said this aloud to myself,) "I'm going to do whatever the fuck it takes to get free." Excuse my language, but that was the truth, I couldn't live like "Go to the hospital, go to the hospital, go to the hospital."

I had never experienced anything quite like that, and it remains my most profound spiritual experience to date. I obeyed. I drove to the hospital, checked myself in at the psych ward, and said, "If you don't help me, I'm walking out of here, and I'm ending it." I got the help I needed that day, and it was the beginning of my healing journey.

The doctor put me on anti-depressants, and after about a week, it was like a light went on. It was like I got my sanity. The anti-depressants truly did help me physically. I think my emotional scale before Prozac was negative 10 to 0. The absence of anxiety was my best day! Somebody else's zero (worst day) was my, "Whew, I'm functioning. Yeah!" (aka my best day).

The drugs put me back into the normal 0-10 scale. I still had emotion. It was just normal emotion, appropriate emotion. It stabilized me internally.

I felt kind of normal for the first time, and it was at that time I thought, (and I said this aloud to myself,) "I'm going to do whatever the fuck it takes to get free." Excuse my language, but that was the truth, I couldn't live like that anymore. I believe that day at the psych ward was the catalyst. There were still eating disorders to come, and different coping mechanisms as well, that would start, and I would have to undo. However, in the process since then, I have never gone back to that place of suicidal thoughts. I made a permanent decision that "I can't ever go back there."

When asked the question as to what resources I have tapped into in my endeavor to find peace and healing, I can honestly say, I've tried it ALL. I encourage others that if you think something might work for you, try it. The first thing I did was decide to look at EVERYTHING. I think I know about God, and the world around me and choose to let it go.

I knew that even if some of what I had come to see or believe about the world was correct, it was still built on such a crooked foundation that the version I was believing had to be somewhat warped. I've had to come up with my own foundational truths I knew that I could stand on, to build a new foundation. These were three truths that I had come to discover as an adult through my own experience, not through another's teaching. There are three things that I know that I know I know in my core; God is good, God is real, and he's bigger than me. That's it. Those are the only things I knew for sure. Knowing this permitted me to let go of a layer of the BS that I was raised with. It also allowed me to begin building, even in the smallest way, a new foundation.

When raised with a lot of chaos and trauma, certain foundational lessons get missed. As a result, as an adult, you have to learn basic things that you never learned when you were a kid. Like faith, trust, joy, love, peace, and more. One of the obstacles I encountered in my process, is that it seems that in a lot of self-help and even psychotherapy, there is this notion that certain concepts and principles are a given.

Let's take "trust," for example. The truth is, as a child of abuse you don't know what the word trust means. You have a basic concept in your mind, but since you've never experienced it, it would be like asking someone born blind to describe the color blue. One has nothing to pull from, and although they could tell you it's a color and give a few facts, you have no real experiential knowledge of the color. Therefore, you can't describe it accurately.

People say, "Oh well, just trust. Let go, believe, etc...," but a child of abuse does not know what that means. It has to be learned. Therefore, I started that process in my relationship with GOD. In the beginning of this process, God would say to me, "Can you trust me for an hour?" I would be like, "I have no idea what that means, and no idea if I can do that." What that meant was, "Can you just not worry and not stress out about everything that you don't have control over, for just one hour?"

I would have to choose to do that. And keep choosing it. Sometimes minute by minute. After about an hour, the stress and the anxiety, would all come rushing back. I'd then have to choose to trust again for an hour. It was baby steps for a long time. Eventually, I got to a place where I could trust for a whole day, and then a week. Now, I have a radically trusting relationship with God. That foundation taught me how to then replicate that same pattern of trust building, in relationships with other people. One of the most tedious parts, but probably the most important part of my actual healing process has been to go back, start over and learn the basics I just didn't know how to do.

The third thing I believe that has profoundly helped me in the last few years is that I permitted myself to do whatever I've had to do to work out my healing. I have stopped trying to please everyone else, or worry about how others will see me as a result of my road. I came to realize that at the end of the day, I'm the only one living this life. Nobody else is inside, nobody else knows what it feels like inside, and if that means I'm sad, I'm sad. If that means I'm angry, I'm angry.

As soon as I did that, permitting myself to embrace the process, allowing myself to be, do, and feel whatever I needed to, life changed. It meant permitting myself to put me first. Permission to let go of things, and relationships that were unhealthy. Even permission to let go of my story, and allow a new one to emerge. That's when I think the really deep healing started to happen. As a result, I am now in a place where the past doesn't rule my life. It isn't what I lead with. I find I don't need to talk about it much anymore. It's not my defining chapter.

If you are just beginning to travel the road of healing, first of all, I would say, "Awesome! Good job! Permit yourself to be on your journey, and to go through whatever process you need to go through to get free. Just surrender to it, because there's not a way over it or around it, it's only through it. Everybody's journey looks different, and I think beating yourself up or judging yourself for what your process looks like only prolongs your process. Nobody else has walked your shoes, so nobody else's process is going to look exactly like yours. Give yourself permission and grace to do whatever you have to do to find yourself and to find your freedom."

Yes, it can be a difficult choice, sometimes, as you choose it. Sometimes it's two steps forward, one step back. There's got to be grace in your process. Setbacks, triggers and overall bad days will happen. Sometimes you're going to have these monumental, "Yes" moments full of victory and breakthrough. Then sometimes you're going to have these, "Why am I still stuck here?" Know that you're not alone in that. Everybody has a level of that going on, even people who haven't been through massive trauma, have a level of that going on. You just don't see it. That's part of the human process. You're not always going to get it right every single time, and it's okay.

The process can and will be frustrating at times. The road to healing is winding, rocky, and unpredictable. Many times, I felt like I was going backward, rather than forwards. But what I know now from hindsight, is that healing is like hiking up a mountain full of switchback trails. As you climb, you walk a path that feels familiar and goes in a similar direction over and over. Each time you are three feet higher on the mountain, three feet farther from your past, and three feet closer to your goal.

You are moving. You are healing. You are getting free, even if at times it doesn't feel that way. Have faith in yourself. Trust your gut; it knows everything you need. Learn to give yourself a voice and by so doing a chance at a better life.

As a cult and abuse survivor, Katie Hulbert is quickly becoming a powerful voice within the self-help community. Having been raised in the shepherding movement, within a family deeply entrenched in church (cult) leadership, she was subjected to years of spiritual, emotional and sexual abuse.

At the age of 25, after an intense battle with suicide and a power encounter with the divine, she started on her healing journey. Her mission now is to empower others to do the same. Her approach, grounded in scientific and spiritual truths, is from the perspective of one who has actually had to walk the road to freedom, one step at a time. As a result, she is a no- nonsense, straight talking and extremely transparent expert on overcoming fear and shame.

You can connect with me at www.shifthappensanyway.com or
www.instagram.com/kthulbert
And get your copy of GURL at
https://www.amazon.com/dp/B07831LWC1
Video Interview: https://youtu.be/3_L4UPbt_pU

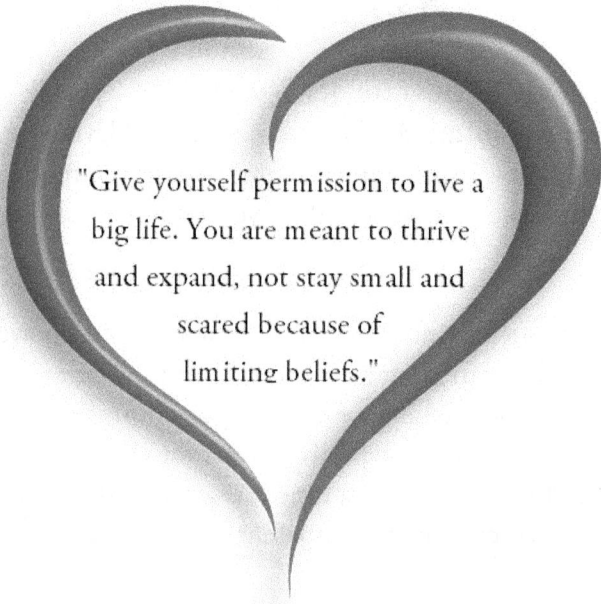

"Give yourself permission to live a
big life. You are meant to thrive
and expand, not stay small and
scared because of
limiting beliefs."

Everything in Life Is a Choice

By Amy Perez

At the age of five, my world changed colors. At that time, my uncle who was six years older than me molested me multiple times. When this occurred, my sexuality opened up. As a young girl, I began to experiment with my body through masturbation, and it also awoke several sexual experiences with my slightly older female cousin.

Like most parents, my parents never thought that anything of this nature would ever happen to their daughter right underneath their nose. Especially being that he was my uncle and they always were very overprotective of me. Nonetheless, when this all began, I felt it was necessary to keep silent because, if my family found out, they would have banned me from visiting my grandma's house. My grandma was someone who was so very special to me, and I didn't want to jeopardize my visits there. Unfortunately, this was also the place where my uncle would have sexual intercourse with me.

I grew up in a very sheltered traditional Mexican home, where I was not allowed to have friends come over, receive phone calls, go to school dances, have slumber parties, or hang out with friends. My parents expected me to attend school and bring good grades only. Due to this, at the age of 14, I met an older guy who was the older brother of one of my female classmates. This girl wasn't a positive influence on me. During the ending of middle school, she would cut school to hang out with her brother and his friends. I was so sheltered, I became friends with her and began ditching school as well. It was the only time that I was able to taste freedom! Over time, I eventually became part of their inner circle and got close to my friend's older brother. Although I was 14 years old and he was 21, he didn't seem to mind me becoming his girlfriend. Other than my early childhood experience with my uncle, this 21 yr old guy was the first person I willingly had sex with.

As time progressed, I began to spiral downward in my life as I became deeply invested in this relationship and a new circle of friends. There was a part of me that enjoyed the adrenaline that came with his dangerous lifestyle, but things began to change drastically, as I started seeing the real him. I was surrounded by drugs, alcohol, blood money, guns, and constant people in and out of his home, buying and selling illegal drugs. In the midst of being surrounded by all these activities, he also began to physically and sexually abuse me.

One night, we were in the living room watching a movie while people were coming in and out of the house as usual. His friends came into the house to do their daily delivery, as usual, he asked me to go into his room while he handled business, but this time instead of doing as I was told, I told him no. With the short fuse he had, he started yelling at me in front of everyone, I then got upset and started yelling back at him. We started arguing and the next thing I knew he grabbed me and started taking me to his room. We were both yelling, I was fighting not to go in the room, and he was pulling me and forcing me into the room.

Once in the room, he slapped me, he pressed me against the wall and started choking me and told me not to forget who was the boss. He then threw me on the bed and tied my hands and feet while taking my clothes off. I was yelling for help knowing there were other people in the house, but no one including his sister came to help. Instead, after he had me naked and tied up to the bed, he walked out the room and left me to which for me felt like forever.

All of the sudden I heard people walking down the hall, the door of his room opened as he and four of his friends coming in all with grins on their faces. I was scared and started shaking, started trying to get my hands and legs free but had no luck. He was the first one to take a turn on me after he was done using me he told his friends to take a turn on me. It didn't matter how much I yelled, or how hard I fought it did nothing. Five guys having fun with my body and no one helped me. I couldn't do anything. After they were all done, he untied me and left me in the room with the light off. The experience changed the color of my world forever.

It took about ten years before I decided to do what it would take to begin healing. I started by going to counseling to talk about my story, to learn how to be vulnerable with my counselor and with myself. I have a lot of work to do still because I'm suffering from the trauma.

I have PTSD, and I have night terrors. Facing my trauma and talking to my counselor has been very helpful in learning how to make peace for myself. Talking about it has helped me with the guilt that I carried, thinking I deserved what had happened to me. Speaking up and doing the work to my healing is changing my life drastically. It has prepared me for a better adult life, and to be a positive influence and role model for my family, and the world. I'm trying to be a better woman, a better mother, a better spouse, and a better friend. I cannot do any of that if I haven't healed myself and made peace with my shadows. I can't be the better version of myself if I'm not willing to put in the work that it takes to become better. To be more, I need to become more. Ultimately the only person who can hold me back or keep pushing me forward is myself.

The most important thing I've done in my healing journey is realizing and accepting that I needed help. Many people will realize they need help but never move forward with accepting or finding the resources that we need to overcome our trauma. Counseling was one of the positive things I did to heal parts of my trauma. Speaking about the traumas and being vulnerable with someone, and hearing my stories spoken out loud helped me heal the many wounds that were still open and bleeding.

With the counseling also came exercises to help me be able to open up about the experience, such as telling my story in the third person. Those are little things that could make a huge impact and difference in the way we see our story. In regards to my uncle, I was able to write him a letter and tell him how all the abuse affected me, how it's affected my relationship with my friends, with my significant others, and with my kids. The letter was to vent, to let him know how I felt, how it's made me feel all these years, to release all the feelings and emotions. I began to OWN those dark feelings and emotions. It opened up a jar of emotions to let him know how he scared me for life, but it also opened up the jar so I could learn to forgive him.

Because now that I have two daughters aged five and six-years-old, I'm always on alert. Where are they going? Who are they going with? Unfortunately, I haven't been brave enough to write a letter to my ex-boyfriend, because I feel like I still have a lot of healing to do with that I'm hoping that the more I talk about it, the more I heal, that soon I will be able to write to him. I know I purposely hold onto that grudge because I'm not ready to forgive him and let go.

I would say to anyone who has gone through dark times and abuse in their lives that you will need to be strong, be vulnerable, find a counselor and a support system. In my case, my support system has been my fiancée. He's helped me with my night terrors; he's the one that pushes me to go to my counseling, he's sat next to me in my counseling sessions, he's been with me 100% of the way.

Finding a counselor I feel helps because you are in a safe environment. You can talk freely, and they are not there to judge you; your counselor is only there to help you. Joining a women's group will be helpful for your healing journey. I found a group here in Arizona called "Woman Within."

In groups like this, you meet other women from all walks of life, and you get to learn their story and experiences, and it dawns on you that you're not alone. There are other women out there who are going through the same or worse experiences than you, and you find support within one another. You find women who not only know what you are going through but also understand you. Unfortunately, my family has not been there for me, but I'm lucky enough to have a man who has been pushing me and supporting me. I now know everything is and will be fine!

For a long time, I put all men under the same umbrella, thinking they were all bad and cold-hearted. However, over time I learned that just because I had a bad experience that does not define how ALL men are. It's like opening a cookie jar and seeing one with melted chocolate chips and broken in half and rock hard! All are the other chocolate chips cookies bad? No, they're not! We just happen to grab the bad one in the jar. Same goes back to my experience, not all men are horrible and closing my heart did no good.

We all want to be loved, accepted, pampered and cared for. When we decide to hide our heart and put it in a safe box, with cement walls, and with electric gates, we don't realize that we are only harming ourselves. That bad experience does not mean you're not going to find your king, your better half, or your missing piece to your puzzle. It's about giving it time, preparing yourself, being patient, we are what we attract. Once we start healing and making peace with ourselves and most importantly start loving ourselves, then we start attracting good people into our life.

We are energy, we radiate energy, and energy is contagious. If you are happy, you're positive, outgoing, and energetic, everyone around you will feel that. However, if you're down and sad, your posture is down, and everyone around you will get contaminated with that energy as well. It's hard when we are going through a rough situation, to keep a positive energy. We have to remember that life is happening for us, not to us.

Having a good support system and pushing yourself to heal, remember that the change you are making is good. Constantly remind yourself that you will have a healthy family, a good heart, and peace knowing that you will make it past these dark times. Everything in life is a choice.

Amy Perez

I am currently working at a law firm, something that I've always wanted to do but never thought I would be doing. It's definitely a new challenge, because it's something that I'm learning from scratch and never been exposed to, but it's helping me grow and nonetheless I am learning so much. I'm very grateful for this opportunity because it just fell on my lap, yet I know it has helped me align myself better with my purpose in life. It feels good to love your job and to look forward to going to work each and every day.

My passion now is helping women and kids who have suffered sexual, physical, and mental abuse. I want to be able to help, save, and educate as many lives as I can. One of my goals is to start a non-profit organization and build shelters all over the world that will provide the resources this women and kids need. Not only will it be a safe place where they have what they need, such as hygiene products, food, and shelter but they will also be provided with psychologists to help them deal with their trauma.

There will be provided with health care, and have groups to help them socialize with other people, like cooking seminars, workout groups, Zumba classes, crochet classes, and even retreats.

I'm working on making more time to volunteer in homes and shelters to give back to the community.

Here is a list of the books I have read that have helped me along my journey:

The Alchemist
Men are From Mars, Women are from Venus
The Prey
How to be a Bawse
The Four Agreements
Soup: A Recipe to Create a Culture of Greatness

Video Interview: https://youtu.be/4FDyVgmv3CY

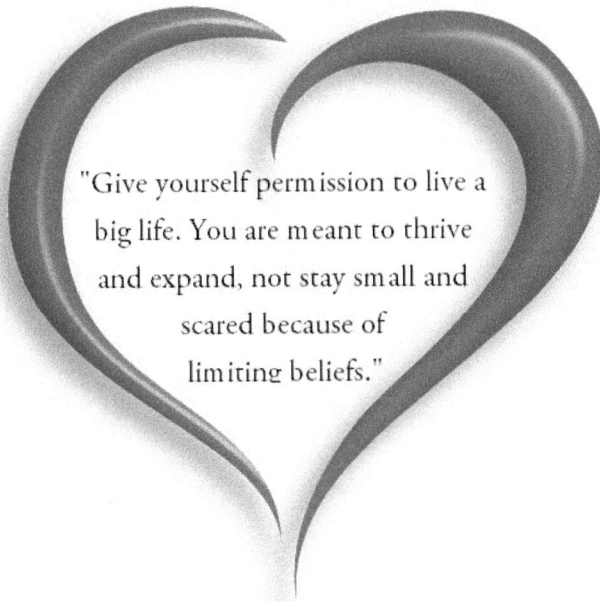

"Give yourself permission to live a big life. You are meant to thrive and expand, not stay small and scared because of limiting beliefs."

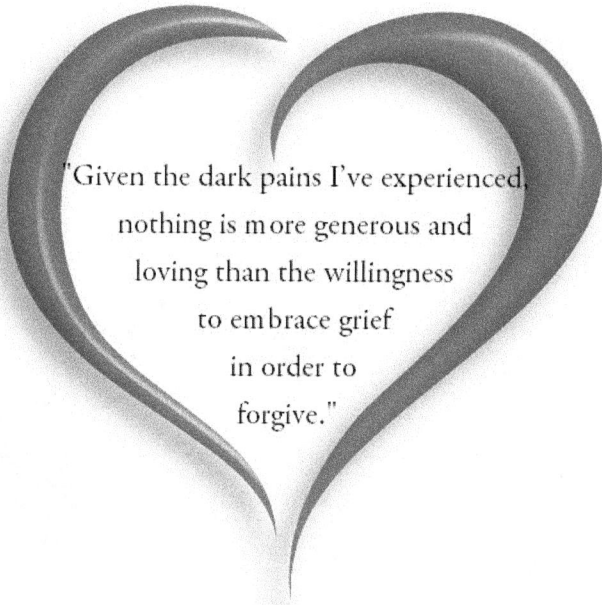

"Given the dark pains I've experienced,
nothing is more generous and
loving than the willingness
to embrace grief
in order to
forgive."

Grace's Story

What is Shame, and How Do People Thrive?

By Shannon O'Leary

*A*fter suffering severe abuse as a child in Australia, I wrote my memoir The Blood on my Hands (O'Leary, 2016). I also shared my feelings and reflections in a chapter of the first book in this series called, We Choose to Thrive (Norwood, 2016).

Subsequently, I have had many people connect with me to communicate their ideas and thoughts about abuse, survival, being a victim and thriving. Most women who shared their stories had an overwhelming sense of shame and anxiety about the abuse and wondered how they could live their lives fully, free from the traumatic memories of the past.

It is for this reason. I have been asking this question; "What is shame, and how do people thrive when they are battling with this toxic emotion?"

"Shame and guilt often go hand in hand, which is why they are often confused. Shame says, "I am bad." Guilt says, "I did something bad." (Burton, 2012)

Over the years, I have been fortunate enough to cross paths with people from many walks of life. Many have told me personal stories with their tales of resilience, bravery, joy, and pain. Other peoples stories have touched on obsession, revenge, forgiveness, and love. Some of these oral histories are etched in my soul because of the power, courage and the honesty in which they were told.

While listening to the stories of women who had experienced trauma, it struck me that there was often a universal underlying emotional theme. Many hurt souls were struggling to come to terms with the all imprisoning emotion called shame. Jung (1934) said that "Shame is a soul eating emotion," and his observations seem all too true. Shame is the powerful emotion that makes us want to cover up our perceived flaws and hide them away from the world.

So where does shame come within the abuse arena? Honestly? It is everywhere. It is in the language that the victims of abuse use; words such as humiliated, embarrassed and degraded, all reflect the painful feeling of distress caused by the loss of self-respect or esteem. In abusive situations, this humiliation exhibits itself through the victim's consciousness of what they perceive as their regrettable behavior. They seem to forget that their behavior was a by-product of someone else's actions. Often, they were in an unfortunate situation where shame was thrust upon them by someone else.

So how can one thrive after an abusive situation? There is no immediate remedy. It can be a personal journey filled with doubt, anger, shame and seemingly bottomless sadness. However, it can also bring happiness, self-revelation, a truce between past and present and eventually, self-acceptance.

To often do we forget that abuse can present itself at any age. Children, teenagers, adults and the elderly can all be subject to abuse, be it physical, emotional or both. Often, the aftermath for these victims is a life filled with shame and an innate desire to stop feeling, to go numb and shut down.

In an age where we are asking people to disclose abuse and its perpetrators in the general community, there lies a group of people who are still harboring memories from a time when abuse was not talked about and thrown into the blackest of cupboards.

These are elderly women over the age of seventy, who have forged their bridges to recovery. For many, this healing came much later in life. With no counseling or help available in their youth, these women tried their best to self-counsel, to bear and live with the pain inflicted upon them. They learned to deflect the hurtful moments while trying to get on with their lives. They dealt with the corrosion of shame and lived in the shadow of its effects. Many of these women disclosed their stories to me in their twilight years, and their memories are as clear as if the events had happened yesterday.

There is one woman in particular, whose story struck a personal chord with me when she shared her feelings of trauma, abuse, and shame.

Grace was an old lady who endured horrific physical abuse as a child from her alcoholic father. We met on the street and struck up a friendship where we would meet for coffee at a shopping center in town. One night, we went to dinner at the local club, and she confided in me in an almost inaudible voice. "I have never spoken of my abuse before," she whispered, and she began to tell me her story.

Grace had carried her trauma with her for ninety-four years and had built a steely wall which she believed was impenetrable. I had spoken briefly of my abuse to her before, and something I had said had finally triggered her wall to collapse.

As a child, Grace had endured countless savage beatings. She had sustained fractures and bruises which were discounted by others because she lived in the post-Victorian Era. Her father belittled and belted her senseless, and she believed she was the cause of his sadistic behavior. In every way, she tried desperately to be the "good girl" she thought he wanted her to be, but deep in her heart, she felt she was a failure and deserved punishment. Her confusion was paramount, which pushed her into the depths of sadness. Her pain-filled shame over-rode all sense and reason. Suicidal thoughts and anger, hellish depressions and anxiety, which she tried to overcome by pushing herself to the brink of physical exhaustion.

Humiliation does this to children. The abuser manipulates the child's emotions so that they confuse the borderlines of whom to trust and love. Their judgment of what is right and wrong is affected. The abuser catapults their self-worth into the world of doubt and shame.

Grace told me she was very clever at hiding her pain. Her family lived on the outskirts of a rural Australian town, and they were very poor. Her mother tried to support the family by chopping wood, despite being subject to severe beatings and emotional torture from her cruel husband. Grace would often run away and hide until dark, but the abuser would find her, and she would be at his mercy.

Grace would wear her school jacket and thick woolen stockings all year round, sometimes in forty degrees heat, to cover the bruises and welts on her body. She went to school with broken fingers, toes and a broken rib, hiding her pain from the world because she believed her condition was her fault. Grace also began to sleep outside, rather than in the house, so her father couldn't find her when he was in an inebriated rage. Her life as a child was lonely and broken, and her soul was filled with shame.

Grace's feelings were intertwined and twisted together like the roots of a tree. As a child, she was manipulated into thinking she was the problem. The shame of feeling she was bad would stay with her and become her shadow in the years to come.

When she disclosed her abuse, her eyes filled with tears, and her hands were shaking. "I am so ashamed," Grace said sadly. I asked her, "Why?" After all, she was not the abuser; she had done nothing wrong.

"The shame I feel," she said. "Is that I could never please my father. I was not the child he wanted. He used me and discarded me like an old rag." Her self-loathing was scathingly apparent. "I have never talked about my childhood," she said, "It is too painful."

The words Grace said, raised the question in my mind as to how was able to thrive despite her feelings of inadequacy and shame. How could one so fragile build upon their shattered self-esteem and function again?

I looked at the woman in front of me, trying to reach an answer. Superficially, her life in the material world seemed fine. She wore a neat white shirt with a vest and long dark pants. She was clean and tidy and rode around taking care of her business on a mobility scooter. Looking into her eyes, I could see Grace's pain. Her blue-veined hands trembled, and she muttered, "Everything is not always as it seems. Sometimes I feel so strong, and at other times, I feel ashamed and broken. I aim to keep busy and active until the day I die." Grace waved her hand as if dismissing the ghosts from the past. "I will not let him win; I am determined to keep living, to keep getting up each day and willing myself to keep going. I am not desperate, and I refuse to be broken."

I wanted to look deeper. I could see that Grace was a survivor who had flourished and lived in the way she felt most comfortable. She had a peace about her and lived and dealt with life's curve balls, in the way she felt could handle them. When she finally allowed me to visit her at her home, she was still struggling with her disclosure. She was frightened of my judging her and that I would tell others about her living conditions.

In her twilight years, Grace had become a hoarder, and the mountain of collected objects had grown and grown until it spilled out into her once spacious yard. In the end, she became ashamed of her home and wouldn't let people visit her. The bathroom in the house became a pile of broken porcelain and pipes, and the walls of her old house began to crumble. The floor collapsed with the weight upon it, and Grace moved a caravan into her yard to live in. When this van filled up with the things she had collected, she moved into another van. There was a makeshift shower in the corner of the yard and wire traps in the bushes and on fences, to deter strangers who might venture on to the property. Grace assured me that she was happy. She had adopted several stray cats and a dog, fed wild birds, and lived on the bread line. "It's like camping, and I can pick my stuff up, get my pets and leave whenever I want."

There were things piled up all around her. There were mountains of newspapers, books, tins and old car parts. In the past, Grace had told me that her father broke everything that was precious to her as a child and I wondered if this was the reason she couldn't bear to throw anything away?

So where is the thriving aspect of the cluttered life Grace kept so well hidden?

Many people looking at her house and surroundings could easily dismiss her as being unwell, but beyond the clutter was an intelligent, well educated and strong woman. She was comfortable in her skin. Yes, Grace had blemishes and still lived with fear, but she was also resilient and kept trying to forge ahead and enjoy life.

I feel Grace thrived by becoming the person that she was. She taught me a lesson and made me understand that people who are abused need to be given affirmation so they can thrive. They need to occasionally hear what they have achieved and congratulated because they have taken giant steps in their lives to stop the abuse cycle.

I told Grace she was an amazing person and that she had survived and thrived after her abuse. Her achievements were many, and her life filled with colorful and courageous memories. Through the telling of her story, Grace finally began to see how far she had traveled down the road to healing. She slowly realized that after her father died, her shame began to dissipate as she took on another life. It hid in the objects she collected and grew on cobwebs in corners. Grace still felt its fangs bite her in moments of darkness, but as the years went on, she learned to push it further away. As time passed, shame became a murky, cloudy feeling that only crept in when she was emotionally vulnerable.

Grace thrived because she battled her feelings of shame and began to build self-confidence through competition. She didn't have to win. Telling herself, she could "do it" getting past the starting line, and finishing were her ultimate goals. When her mother was alive, Grace had a relationship which never faltered. The strength of this bond was exemplified in the1950's, when they both entered the Redex Trials (an Australia car reliability trial run on some of the toughest roads and conditions in the world), a thing which women were rarely seen to do at that time.

Grace also went to weekly band practice, was in several brass bands and entered multiple competitions all over the country. She attended poetry meetings and busked in the streets playing her harmonica and mandolin. Despite other competitors laughing at her (she was very small in stature and used a child's bow and arrow), Grace won the gold medal at seventy years of age for archery in the Senior Games. She could shoot a rifle and win carnival prizes, play the harmonica and be a protagonist at council meetings. Grace also adopted several stray cats and dogs and housed them, and taught herself about unconditional love.

Grace thrived because she became comfortable in her own skin. She accepted herself, warts and all. She was self-sufficient, incredibly strong-willed, forthright and honest. She became a music teacher and mastered many instruments. She made bush remedies to heal sick friends, and she was kind to others. Grace would fight and hiss like a feral cat if she thought someone was unjust, making it her place to fight for the underdog who was treated unfairly.

In many ways, her father's death had liberated her. At first, when he died she would whisper "I am glad he is dead." As her life progressed, it became clearer to her, some of the shame had died with him because most of it was about him, not herself.

Grace never totally overcame shame, but she battled it and learned self-acceptance. She deeply believed that it was wrong for a father to give the gift of life, and then snatch it away again by draining and destroying their child's self-esteem. "I have learned to live with shame," she said. It is not my friend or my enemy. Shame and I have made a truce."

It is easy for others to make social comments like, "Don't be sorry or ashamed of the past, it is over so forget it." The truth is that shame cuts into a person's soul too deeply. It is sometimes so overwhelming the victim becomes immobilized. It often creeps up on victims, berating them for something that they had no control over; and these feelings of shame tell their psyche and self-esteem they are worthless.

To thrive, an abused person must remember that they were a pawn in the psychopaths game, and they were a victim, and are innocent. Recovery is a hard road because memories are often ever present. Sometimes, shame is violent and comes in flashes. It chips and chops up self-esteem and wears even the hardiest of souls down. It is good to remember, but it also can be really painful. Sometimes memories cause shame, and they suffocate and claw at reason. To thrive, one has to try and plow through the quagmire and remember past is past.

Stephen Fry (2003) wrote about shame and what he said burns true for many; *"Heightened self-consciousness, apartness, an inability to join in, physical shame and self-loathing– they are all not bad. Those devils have been my angels. Without them, I would never have disappeared into language, literature, the mind, laughter and all the mad intensities that made and unmade me."*(Fry. 2003)

We can all learn an inspiring lesson from Grace's story. In her, we see that the fragility of old age can be inter-mixed with inner durability and resilience. She chose to thrive after years of abuse and became friends with herself again. Her shame was put on the back burner, and although it lurked in the past, she won the race against it and tried never to let it win.

References:

Burton, N. (2012), Hide and Seek United kingdom: Acheron Press.

Jung, C. G. (1934), Nietzsche's Zarathustra, James L. Jarrett, ed. Princeton, NJ: Princeton University Press. 1988

Fry, S. (2003), Moab Is My Washpot, An Autobiography, New York: Soho 1997.

O'Leary, S. (2016) The Blood on my Hands, USA: Amazon Books

Norwood, B. (2016) We Choose to Thrive, USA: Amazon Books.

Shannon O'Leary

Shannon O'Leary is a prolific writer and performer. She is the author of several books of poetry and children's stories, and she has won many awards for song-writing. Shannon O'Leary is the Australian author of the powerful memoir The Blood on my Hands (Amazon Books). Set in 1960s and '70s Australia, The Blood on My Hands is the dramatic tale of Shannon O'Leary's childhood years. O'Leary grew up under the shadow of horrific domestic violence, sexual and physical abuse, and serial murder. Her story is one of courageous resilience in the face of unimaginable horrors.

O'Leary has acted and directed on the stage and on Australian national TV, and currently manages her production company and music studios. She has numerous graduate and post-graduate degrees in education, music, and science and believes that through education and positive support and kindness from others, a person's life can take a turn for the better.

"I come from the School of Most Fortunate" she says, "Because I have been lucky enough to survive my past."

Shannon also was a co-writer in the first book of the We Choose to Thrive series and is honoured to take part in this sequel. She is a teacher and academic, has five children with her deceased former husband, and lives with her longtime partner in Sydney, Australia.

Video Interview: https://youtu.be/LuCfSpcLS3k

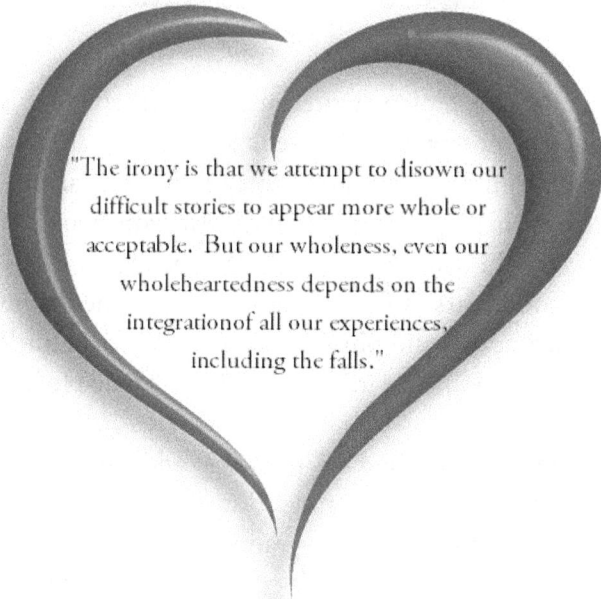

"The irony is that we attempt to disown our difficult stories to appear more whole or acceptable. But our wholeness, even our wholeheartedness depends on the integrationof all our experiences, including the falls."

Brene Brown

Who Wins When You Do?

By Maddie Caballo

It started from birth for me. I was born into a family that belonged to a group. As near as I can gather, I was probably born to be given to other people. I did not know anything other than abuse during my childhood. There was a lot of torture, including physical, mental, and sexual abuse. I lived that way until I was twenty years old. That is when I finally found my way out.

When I was about thirteen years old, one of the people in our group was caught abusing me at school. That individual went to trial, and I was a witness in the courtroom and testified against this person.

I did live in a group home for a period of time, but my parents still had custody of me, so they would still pick me up and bring me back into the awful environment. My abuse revolved around a calendar system that they had created. There were days that very important to them. During that time they had established rituals. Sometimes there were small groups of people, and other times there were larger groups that participated in the abuse.

Being raised in this kind of environment, breaking away as I became an adult led to an entirely different set of circumstances. For a time, I attracted what I knew. It has been very difficult for me to learn to live in a different environment.

I am 46 years old now, and I still feel like I'm learning every day to belong in a world that operates in a much different way both in thinking and mindset. Even though I have been away from that environment for many years, because my formative years were so damaging, both to my mind and body, I still find I have difficulty in some areas of my life. It has been quite the learning process.

As I entered adulthood, I didn't know how to just be. I did not have a normal frame of reference. I had to learn in adulthood things I should have learned in childhood.

I ended up marrying somebody who was a good, safe person because that was all I was looking for. I was very clear while we were dating that I would not tolerate any form of abuse. But the truth is, the relationship was void of the other things I needed in a relationship and the marriage ended up not working out.

I was still learning so much and didn't know how to take care of myself. I ended up being assaulted on the way to work early one morning. That is when I was triggered into seeking some deep healing therapy work on my past.

Being able to talk about it now is healing as well. Simply knowing that I was not the only one to experience something of this nature, and being able to share my story in the hopes of someone else finding healing, makes life better.

Healing is a journey. I've been in therapy the assault happened. I go two or three times a week. It helps me to stay capable of functioning more healthily. My current therapist describes me as incapable of making eye contact, I would keep my head down, and my hair would cover my face. I had difficulty sharing details of my past even though I had been seeing another therapist for seven years.

Now, with her expert guidance, I can share my story, and I have gained so much more confidence. There are still hard days when something triggers me when emotions find me or I find them, but it keeps getting better and better. I am not always comfortable talking about my past, but I am becoming so much more able to sit with my emotions now. For so long, it was not safe to express emotions. I could not express pain; I could not cry. It simply was not safe, and I had learned to keep my emotions tight inside of me. Now I'm learning it is safe to release them.

It's a journey I find the need to be diligent with, and sometimes I feel like I am going backward. Talk therapy has helped. So has cognitive behavioral therapy. My current therapist combines EMDR with equine therapy.

I feel that the equine therapy has helped me the most and has made the biggest difference in healing a being able to move forward. As I began to learn to trust the horse, I was able to start setting boundaries, asking for what I needed. I was able to learn social skills more safely. Humans had hurt me. It has been very difficult to trust humans.

When I go to the arena, as I worked and built a connection with the horses, I began to feel myself grow as a person. Now, I have my horses, I live on my alone, and have a small farm. I am happy.

What I would say to anyone struggling to find their way after abuse of any kind: Reach out for help! Maybe the first person, or even the first few, won't be right for you. Don't let that stop you.

Some people use art; others use writing, or dance, yoga or meditation. I use animal-assisted therapy. There is no right or wrong way.

Whatever it is, whatever it takes, find the right person, or the right venue that suits your needs. Something my work for awhile and then you outgrow it, or it does not suit your current needs. Actively seek what works to keep you living a better life. The road is not always easy.

The fact you are reading this book is a good sign. You can also watch my video interview. Know you are NOT alone. There are a good many of us out there that know the journey. You are a beautiful example of someone who knows the journey and is willing to do what it takes.

I used to think I could erase that part of my life. I cannot. Nor can you. It will always be with you. When I realized that, my choice was to become a part of a sisterhood that supports other women coming out of the horrible memories of their past. Abuse is abuse, no matter what the abuse is. Seek ways to heal. Who wins when you do? YOU!

"She couldn't feel her wings,
but she knew they were there.
So she built a ladder to the sky,
and when she touched the
clouds, whe would
remember how
to fly."

~Atticus

Maddie Caballo

Maddie Caballo is an Education/Equine Facilitated Learning Specialist with over 25 years of experience working in the field of education. She has developed curriculum, specialized in accreditation, and assisted over 12,000 students to reach their personal goals. Through her own trauma recovery work, she discovered the powerful experience that occurs when you take the learning to the paddock with the horses. The combination of her education experience with her training in equine facilitated learning creates a powerful learning opportunity for clients.

Maddie is certified through O.K. Corral as an Equine Assisted Learning (EAL) professional. She has taken course work towards a certification in Equine Assisted Learning at Prescott College in Prescott, Arizona, and is a Level 2 Graduate in the Parelli Natural Horsemanship program. The most significant training comes from her own personal experience of healing trauma as an on-going client who participates in therapeutic sessions with a therapist who specializes in trauma for many years to heal Dissociative Identity Disorder (DID) and Complex Post-Traumatic Stress Disorder (C-PTSD).

Maddie is now a speaker at national conferences sharing her own personal experience. She understands that she cannot change what happened to her; and now, it is her mission to help professionals working with trauma clients to understand their unique needs. She also seeks to inspire other survivors to continue their journey and search for what feels right for them and know that they are not alone.

"In order to benefit from the healing power of your story, you must resist from holding anything back. It is time to strip off the mask, forget what everyone else will think or say and tell it like it is without apology."

Stay Active with a Good Support System

By Barbie Barton

Some fifteen years ago I was hit by a car. Flying five feet into the air, I suffered a mild traumatic brain injury. I hope I can share my story in a way that will make sense for you.

My abuse began shortly after marriage. My ex-husband had just come out of rehab for prescription drugs. He was addicted to a very powerful muscle relaxant that was worse than heroine. One day, after an argument, I decided to go for a walk so I could cool down. When I returned, he was still angry and kicked me to the ground.

Whenever he was high on his medication, he would get this way. The drugs triggered his explosive anger. Another time, he chased me around the house with a kitchen knife. At the time we lived in a mobile home, and as I raced out the glass door, I was praying for strength as he kept hitting the glass with the knife, making stabbing motions. I called 911 frightened that they would not get to me in time.

When they did arrive, they took him to the hospital. He became uncontrollably angry there. I sought help from the crisis center and while they urged me to leave him, I refused to because he apologized and I knew

43

it was drug induced. I hoped he could get help to kick the habit. They released him, and the abuse continued.

He started mixing the drugs with alcohol and upon discovering a big bottle of vodka, I poured it down the toilet. I then left to go to my doctor appointment. When I returned, he was beyond angry and began pounding on my head and scratched at my eyes. Trying to call for help, he grabbed me around my neck. When I finally reached 911, he was screaming into the phone that I was the "crazy one!"

As a Christian woman, I felt it was my obligation to do all I could to save our marriage, which is why I took him back. I thought I could reach his heart. Finally, I decide to make a break after he fractured my left shoulder blade in one of fits of rage. I was finally done, because I understood that at some time, he could kill me. I suffer now from PTSD and anxiety issues.

My emotional and mental healing has been a journey that has taken some time, but I work hard to stay positive and even help others to realize that they can heal too. I still have my bad days and my good days. When I moved out, I went to Survivors, Inc in Gettysburg. Now I live on my own and doing well.

I find I need to take one day at a time, because it can too overwhelming otherwise. I still have a lot of health issues from my accident, so there are times when is a struggle. However, I find it important to find and stay active with a good support system. I belong to several facebook groups and I actively share positive quotes and try to be there for others as they are coming out of the same type of situation that I was in.

Barbie Barton

I'm now in a great relationship and it's healthy. I'm still getting used to it. I still have my good and bad days as far as my PTSD goes.

I share inspirational words and pictures on social media as a way to give back.

Video Interview: https://youtu.be/fYyPejiuBYM

"Faith is like wi-fi...
it is invisible, but it has
the power to connect you
to what you need."

My Journey of Self Discovery

By Mariana Caceres

"*M*amma, please don't leave me!!! Please, I will do anything, I will be a good girl mamma, please love me!!!" I can still hear my screams of desperation, my voice hoarse and scratchy from my pleading out, from my begging her not to leave me. I thought I was going to pass out, my vision in and out as I gasped only enough air to continue screaming. My knuckles turned white as I held on for dear life to the bars of my gallery gate, as I saw her leave.

As my screams filled up the quietness of the day, my neighbor came outside, and without even checking on me (I imagine she must have sensed the urgency of the situation) ran after my mother. After what felt like an eternity, my neighbor brought my mother back home.

I still do not know what my mother must have been thinking. It must have been terrible. But what I do know, is the trauma it brought to me. This is my journey of self-discovery and how I decided to break the cycle and begin to recreate my life.

I spent my early years in the Caribbean. I lived with my parents, and even though I had siblings (they didn't live with me). I was raised mostly by myself, and I was very shy, quiet and careful with what I would say. I was one of those children that knew too much, for I had learned to walk on eggshells since very early on. I want to say before I move any further with myself, and I was very shy, quiet and careful with what I would say. I was one of those children that knew too much, for I had learned to walk on eggshells since very early on. I want to say before I move any further with my story that my parents did the best they could with the abilities that they had.

Our parents will teach you what they have learned based on their understanding of life. I love my parents and have forgiven them for any pain that they didn't know they were causing. Sometimes their pain is so strong, their nightmares so real, that they will project that onto you unwittingly. Our parents not only give us their physical traits but some of their traumas as well. I guess this is where the term baggage comes from. We say, "oh, this person has baggage from a previous relationship," but in reality, often it is not from a previous relationship, it's from your childhood.

Back to my story, I grew up in constant fear that anything I did would cause my parents to leave me. The love that I received was conditional on my good behavior. It depended on how well I was able to hide my true self. It didn't matter how well I behaved; it was never good enough, I was never good enough. As I look back at my life, I can see how these beliefs kept replaying in my life. I see how some events in my life created patterns that would continue to manifest in my life until I chose to stop the patterns. I had picked up these limiting beliefs in my programmable age (we'll get to that later).

At a young age, I had been sexually abused by a close family member. I remember speaking about what had happened, and nothing was done about it. If anything, I was the one in the wrong, and the beliefs that I didn't matter, I was not loved, I was not good enough kept on cementing themselves in me. These beliefs became part of my subconscious (your subconscious mind runs 95% of your life, which means your life is a photocopy of it). I repressed this particular event, and I would say that I also repressed the feelings attached to them, for when this memory came back, the grief came with it too.

As an adult, I was in a psychologically abusive relationship, and I held on to that relationship for many years. I was starving for love; I felt like I was lucky to have found an attractive man that was interested in me! And if he left me, who was then going to love me? So I stayed and prayed and prayed. I would often cry myself to sleep and wondered what had I ever done so bad, to deserve all the pain I experienced, why couldn't I just be happy. Why doesn't anyone love me? Why doesn't anyone want to stay?

I would work so hard at being liked; I would completely forget about myself, simply to please others so they would stay. But the story would keep on repeating itself, over and over I went breakup after breakup, disappointment after disappointment. At this point, I had gotten to the conclusion that there are just some people that are not meant to know happiness, it is what it is!

So I focused on work & taking care of my parents. Work gave me satisfaction because it would make me feel like I was needed so that I would give it my all and then some. I started getting noticed and began to get promoted. For the first time in my life I started to feel like I mattered, if all these people looked up to me and wanted to be coached by me, it must mean that I wasn't that bad after all. It felt like work was all I had, I was work!!! If nothing else, it was at least a place where I could be myself without any judgment.

The huge amount of crazy hours started to take a toll on my body, and on my personal life. My father had been battling Alzheimer's for a couple of years, and not being able to see me daily (due to my work schedule) affected his memory of me. The first time I realized he didn't know who I was, was tragic for me. My health spiraled so far down that I ended up quitting my job. It was the craziest thing I have ever done! I quit my job without a backup! I quit who I thought I was!!! To quit the only thing that made me feel accomplished was terrifying. Almost two years after that, my father went to heaven (and I would need a separate book to be able to try to explain the pain of losing my honorable warrior), and then the anxiety attacks started.

My anxiety attacks were getting so out of hand that it was almost impossible to continue keeping them hidden. Everything I had ever gone through, I had kept mostly private. I was the provider; I was the strong one, my job was to keep shit together and provide support. It felt like I had been carrying the weight of the world on my shoulders, and it had finally managed to break my back. After another debilitating breakup and extreme pain & anguish at home, I hit rock bottom.

I was floating in a sea of pain, I no longer knew where pain ended, and I started. It was all one; I didn't think I could go on, why would I want to go on anyway? Why did God insist on keeping me here? What is my purpose? Was I just here to take care of people and never be taken care of myself? I could no longer live this way!!!

I cannot tell you exactly what sparked my decision. I don't know if it was finding a specific article, if someone said something, or if perhaps was a combination of things, but one day I said to myself, "other people have gone through worse, and they have made it out!!! I can do it too." I would change my life, even if I died trying! I knew I deserved better, so I set out on the quest to find myself.

Google and YouTube became my best friends. I started researching my symptoms like a crazy woman! I studied information on the inner child, did work on it on myself and by myself. I was no longer scared; I didn't have anything to lose anyway. I found a good therapist that introduced me to subconscious work, and then the changes slowly started.

I am still on this journey. I wouldn't say that I am finished and finally out, but what I can say is that my life has done a complete 360 since last year. There are still days when I feel like I can't go on, and there are situations that I wish were better, but everything has a gestation period, and, I believe that my life is improving every day. I will share below some of the most important information I have come across in the hopes that you can also benefit from it. I will also share some of the authors and techniques used.

I believe that one of the most important things to understand is how our brain works! Without getting too technical and scientific, your mind is separated into two categories: our conscious mind and our subconscious mind.

Your conscious mind is your thinking mind, it's in charge of making decisions, paying attention, it's your creative mind, and it controls your voluntary actions.

Your subconscious mind is your autopilot; it's what keeps your heart beating, your digestion running. It's what has your fingers typing that phone number automatically even when you can't consciously remember it. Your subconscious does everything that you consciously wouldn't be able to remember to do. Imagine if we had to consciously remember to keep our hearts beating! We wouldn't last a minute! Our attention span is terrible! However, that's not the only job it has.

Our subconscious is a recording machine that plays out in our lives everything that it has stored. So, our life is a photocopy of whatever is stored in our subconscious.

Think of it as a computer, or a smart-phone. A smart-phone cannot do anything without having apps being downloaded onto them first. We are the same; when we are in our mother's womb, we start absorbing our environment, we "encode" our mothers strongest feelings, her anxieties, for example, we pick up our father's fears & frustrations. Once we are born, we need programming to help us become integrated into society, so we pick up behaviors from the people around us.

From when we are in the womb to about the age of 7, our brain operates at very low vibrational frequencies, allowing us to pick up all types of programming without much resistance. When we are in those low vibrational frequencies, our conscious mind is not fully developed therefore everything goes straight into the subconscious mind.

Our subconscious mind is mostly not ours, so haven't you ever wondered why you read so many self-help books and try your darn hardest to change but nothing much happens? Our life is being dictated not by what you consciously want, but by whats stored in there. For example, every time I would be threatened as a child to be left, and not loved created a program in me (belief) that would continuously play itself in people abandoning me or putting me in situations where I feared abandonment.

Scientific research proves that we have over seventy thousand thoughts in one day, and out of those seventy thousand thoughts, ninety percent of them are negative (based on negative subconscious programming). If you want to know which ones you might have, just look at your life and see what you are having trouble with. We are vibrational beings and if you are into Quantum Physics like I am, you would by now know that we are pure energy!

Have you ever heard the saying, think positive thoughts and positive things will happen? Think of your brain like a tuning fork, you set the tuning fork at a particular vibration, and when you tap it, will only resonate with another tuning fork set at that exact vibration. If your subconscious is set at a negative frequency, that's all you are going to attract.

So what do we do? You have to start reprogramming your mind with what you desire. Your conscious and subconscious learn in different ways since our subconscious is the autopilot, the habitual mind, it learns by repetition.

1. Create a habit. You can do positive affirmations, but you have to be consistent because your conscious mind will fight you at the beginning.

2. Listen to subliminal messages, or create your own! Subliminal audio is a track where you only consciously hear music, but below the music is a hidden layer of affirmations. These work faster than creating a habit because the affirmations go straight to the subconscious without your conscious mind blocking them (your conscious mind can't hear it, but your subconscious does).

3. Hypnosis, this type of work brings your brain waves down (how we originally program ourselves) and by doing that allows new information to be added to your subconscious.

4. The Emotion Code by Dr. Bradley Nelson. His work allows you to eliminate from your body, trapped emotions that have remained stuck from previous traumas & pains. These trapped emotions sometimes are even carried over from our parents and descendants, causing us great emotional & physical pain, even disease!

The Emotion Code is one of many new healing modalities that have come forward under the continuous studies of energy. Some of the other modalities include EFT, Psych-k, Faster EFT, and The Wonder Method.

Now that we have covered a little bit about how our brain works, we need to touch base on something else. It might be a tough pill to swallow, but we need to learn to forgive and release. Not necessarily forget but release. Some of us have gone through truly terrible things in our life, and it hurts!

Forgive them! Most importantly, forgive yourself and release all that pain that no longer serves you. The more you regurgitate the scenes, the more you cement them in your subconscious. And on top of that, the more you relive it, and feel that pain, the more your body becomes addicted to that feeling!

You can become addicted to your thoughts and you can (just like a drug addict) become addicted to your pain, and the more you knock your body out of balance (because your body would be on survival mode and not on normal mode), the more you are headed for some type of disease.

Some of the resources I would recommend for your journey are as follows:
- If you can, find a good therapist, someone who you feel comfortable with.
- Learn how to meditate, read and start writing.
- Create affirmations and say them to yourself in the mirror, or record yourself and listen to them every day.
- For inner child trauma research, I found a YouTube page by a former doctor named Gerlach.

Some of my favorite authors and YouTubers are:
- Dr. Joe Dispenza (his book, "Breaking the Habit of Being Yourself"

is amazing).
• Dr. Bruce Lipton, he explains things in a very easy to understand format.
• Gregg Braden, his work is remarkable.
• The pioneer of self-love, Louise Hay
• I watched a film called E-motion, I would recommend it to everyone. It is what introduced me to the Emotion Code. It further explains how almost anything can be traced back to trapped emotions and unprocessed experiences.

My journey is not complete, and neither is yours. Whatever it is that you have gone through, you can overcome. You are wonderfully, and perfectly made, and you come fully loaded to be able to achieve everything you set your mind to do.

It is my ultimate wish that my journey and learnings can help you in one way or another. Always remember, you are loved, you are beautiful, you are enough, and there is absolutely nothing wrong with you! You can do this! I believe in you!!!

Many, many wonderful blessings,
Mariana C

Mariana Caceres

Mariana's Video Interview: https://youtu.be/KbfuWPyozb4

Mariana Caceres spent most of her childhood in between Puerto Rico & the Dominican Republic before settling down in her native New York. After taking a creative class in school, Mariana discovered that there was another world in books, one where she could submerge & transport herself to.

Her fascination for the arts continued until the very lives she read about started to make her question her very own. Books took her through her 10 years of retail management until they could take her no further.

It was her time to write her own & in the very essence of it to start to write her new life story.

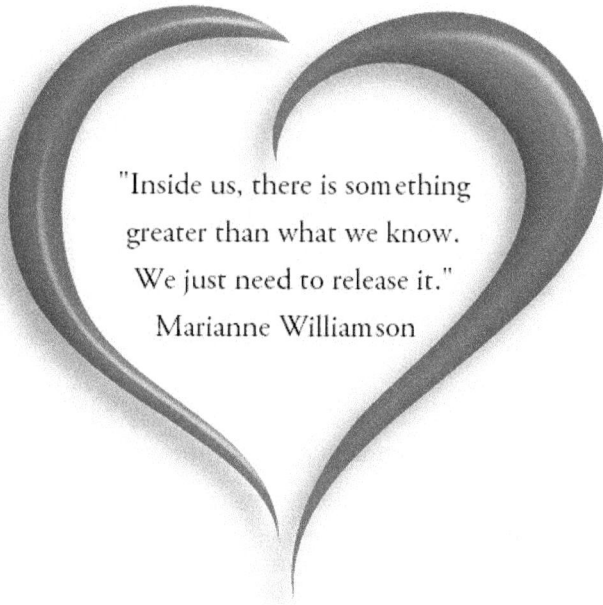

"Inside us, there is something
greater than what we know.
We just need to release it."
Marianne Williamson

#*I'm A Statistic*

By Marissa Cohen

*A*s a survivor, I wanted to take all the negative things that have happened to me in my life, and turn it into a positive. I chose to thrive. I wanted to use those experiences to help other people who have also gone through similar experiences.

One of the most important things that I think, we can do as survivors, is to speak out about it. There is a larger number of survivors than anybody knows, because the statistics show that only about 5% of them are reported. And I know that I never reported, so I'm part of that 95%. I think that by speaking out and being able to tell our stories, and know that we are supported by millions of other people who have also experienced similar things, it's empowering. It's empowering to know that you're not alone. It's empowering to know that you have a network of people behind you who have also dealt with it, who are also willing to help you. And by speaking about it, we're showing people that there is strength in it and strength in numbers.

When I was 19, my first boyfriend in college was physically, psychologically, verbally, and sexually abusive to me. I remember the exact date, January 15, 2010. We were at his house, and I was supposed to leave to go home so I wouldn't miss my curfew. He wanted me to stay and cuddle. I had a few extra minutes, so I told him I'd stay. He told me if I want to stay and cuddle for my last fifteen minutes I'm there, then we have to cuddle naked, which wasn't an unusual thing for us.

For me, who had never had sex and never had any experience with it, that was incredibly intimate for me. And the next thing I knew, he rolled me onto my back, held my hands down and he was raping me. I was in total shock. I couldn't breathe. I couldn't move. I don't even know how long it lasted. But I know that when he was finished, he rolled over and laid on his back, and was incredibly satisfied, panting and heavy breathing, like "oh I worked so hard and did such an amazing job," and I was laying there still in shock. I couldn't even process what just happened to me.

I didn't realize you could get raped by a boyfriend. I thought rape was some stranger jumps out of the woods, rapes you, and then leaves. So for me, being sexually abused by a boyfriend, who I thought I loved, was traumatic. It was a huge violation of my personal space and my privacy, but I couldn't express that because I didn't think that what happened was wrong. I thought that I'm just supposed to have sex with him. I thought that was just part of the deal.

I ended up rolling over and crying for an hour, and missing my curfew, and calling my mom in hysterics telling her that I'm late and I was so sorry, but I couldn't drive. And she told me it was fine and to just stay over at his house. I went home in the morning, and she pretty much validated that sex is a beautiful thing, and it's something you do with someone you love, and that's okay. I didn't tell her that I didn't want to have sex. She was just trying to make me feel better.

Make sure you're safe. Don't just leave and run away and think about never coming back, because what could end up happening is, you get yourself in a predicament where you have to go back, and it could be worse. Or maybe, if you aren't planning ahead, making sure that all of your bases are covered, you could potentially be putting yourself in a more unsafe position. Now, I'm definitely not recommending people stay. That is not what I want. I want everyone who is in an abusive situation or abusive relationship to get out. And I want them to go far and be prepared and be safe. But I also want them to have a safety plan. Because if they don't have a plan, they could be causing more harm. And ultimately, that could be worse for them, or they may end up in a worse situation. So just be prepared. Prepare yourself. It isn't easy. Reach out to any and every resource possible. Ask advice from people. Talk to people. Talking is what is going to keep you safe and alive.

As far as the healing process goes, I'm a huge advocate for talking about it. I'm also a huge advocate for domestic violence and sexual assault survivors. That's what I do. But I think that talking about it and feeling comfortable, finding someone that you're comfortable talking with about it, who will validate you and won't question you is what is important. It may be a best friend or someone from survivor groups online. The people from the survivor groups are the most supportive, because they've gone through it too, and have a more connected understanding of what you're going through, as opposed to people that haven't gone through it), etc., is incredibly therapeutic.

I never reported my assault, and I didn't even acknowledge it until six months later. We broke up two months after he raped me. I didn't speak about it until one random day; I was driving with my best friend. We were jamming out to Taylor Swift and eating candy, and all of a sudden she said something like, "can we stop and get ice cream? If you love me you'll do it", and it triggered me. Even though he never said that, at least that I remember, it triggered me into a full panic attack. I had never had one before. I started hyperventilating; I couldn't breathe. She had to grab the wheel and pull us to the shoulder because I was going to crash. I couldn't control my body.

She turned to me and was like, what the heck just happened to you? Where did that come from? And I told her that he did something to me that I didn't want to do. I didn't want this to happen. I'm trying to fight to figure out why I feel so empty and out of control and vulnerable all the time. I dug deep and explained everything to her. And as soon as I did, I felt so liberated. I felt so liberated afterward because I knew that I could talk finally talk about it.

I own a nonprofit called, "Within Your Reach." We advocate for domestic violence and sexual assault survivors, and we advocate in various ways. We conduct training for advocates to standardize the quality of care that survivors get in hospitals, police departments, etc. We educate in the community. We work with all faiths, youth centers, community centers, and youth groups, etc. We explain the dangers of sexual assault and domestic violence, resources available, etc. But one of the specific problems I'm working on through the NPO and collaborating with other NPO's around the country is called, #ImAStatistic.

The idea of being a part of a statistic typically has a negative connotation. People think that being a statistic makes them a number, a cog in the machine. But truthfully, there is so much power in numbers that nobody has tapped into yet. If 1.5 million girls are raped in colleges every year, and none of those girls speak up, that's 1.5 million people that feel like their alone.

That's 1.5 million people! That's a huge number and a huge statistic. If all of those people ban together, they outnumber the number of people that are doing the raping and the assaulting. So, if all of those people find they are not alone, embrace that they are part of that statistic, and become empowered by being a part of that statistic, I feel that we might be able to end the stigma and also end the silence.

Marissa Cohen

Marissa F. Cohen is the bestselling author of "Breaking Through the Silence; the Journey to Surviving Sexual Assault;" Owner and Executive Director of Within Your Reach, Inc., a nonprofit devoted to helping survivors break the silence and love themselves; and Co-Founder of #ImAStatistic.

Marissa also works with military, veterans and their families to aid in mental health services. She loves traveling the world, and exploring all different cultures.

Her favorite food group is Mac n' Cheese, and scours the United States as a self-proclaimed Mac n' Cheese and Wing Connoisseur. As a survivor, she feels empowered to help other survivors find the peace of mind that she found after her assaults.

www.withinreachil.org
www.imastatistic.org
www.facebook.com/WithinYourReachOrg/
https://www.facebook.com/ImAStatistic/
Marissa's Video Interview: **https://youtu.be/SpeN_XG7I4s**

"It takes more courage and strength to walk
away from a bad situation than to stay in it.
Staying is familiar, no matter how bad it is.
Walking away is stepping into
the unknown, and uncharted
waters."
Becky Norwood

The Fractured Family Syndrome

By a Courageous Contributor

I was the oldest of nine children, and my younger sister is dead. We were very close in age and other ways. We looked alike, had the same tone of voice too. She died in January 2009 and was only forty-one years old.

I have six brothers and one other sister. They are all great people, but the best one is dead. Half her life-span swiped away because she was kind and fine and good. She is dead directly as a result of the abuse, it was put across as having something to do with drink and all that, but there was a lot of programming and abuse by my mother in cooperation with my father. My father did not enable, he cooperated.

I had only come to terms with his part in the process that led directly to her death recently because, my denial before I accepted this, protected me. It was easier to blame my mother for it all, but I now know that there is a pair of them. I also now know that I was very vulnerable to the same tactics that killed my sister which is why I have decided to stay away from the pair of them completely for health and safety reasons to facilitate and accelerate my recovery.

As a child, I used to argue with my mother to protect my siblings. She wanted to fight, and I fought back, to give her an argument to keep her on her feet for her relief, and mainly to protect the rest of them. It was totally against my nature to do that, and it had a bad effect on me.

As the eldest, I had a lot of responsibility from a very young age for caring for my younger brothers and sisters. As time went on, myself and all my siblings were encouraged to focus, succeed, achieve, overwork, be perfect, (all that stuff) and in the context of that, my mother was very controlling in her approach to each of us. She would deliberately say things that would have put us wrong. She was deliberate as bad an example as she could be to me, to lead me astray.

She always had a double standard. She sabotaged, not just with me, but the rest of my siblings as well, to the point that we were all abused people. I thought there was something wrong with me. I was convinced of that. I was programmed like that. She was so cruel to my sister who died, all in the context of pretending to care for her while she actually enjoyed the abuse. This is what actually happened. My father? He played along to save his own skin because he was previously her target for her jealous rage.

I will not give details for two reasons. I don't have to prove anything because the facts are as they are and it would not be of benefit to my recovery to go over it all. Suffice to say; it was all done, deliberately and with malice, and forethought, and then some.

In simple arithmetic terms, there were ten of us including my father at one time and only one of her. If he'd of had the courage to stand up to her (like I did as a child) instead of cooperating with her, my sister would be alive and thriving today.

The facts are, they come across as pillars of the community in this small, rural town but they only have a front, and they are welcome to it!

My mother crosses all gender and family role boundaries because of her craving for power. She thought I was put on this earth solely to keep manners on her. She programmed my lovely sister to misbehave herself

64

into an early grave to make herself feel and look good. She has only one fault really; she prefers a (family) funeral to a wedding.

These are strong words, based on my experience and knowledge of her gained over the years, but her party is over.

I thought that I would simply take some time out from both of them, but as I continue my recovery, this complete estrangement from them feels right, and I am getting better on an hourly, daily basis.

Dealing with that survivor guilt is enough without being sucked into their vacuum for them to repeat history with me as the target this time. My husband and two sons want and need me to be well and happy. My siblings need me to lead by example to improve their quality of life too.

This estrangement is permanent. There are simply too many people's welfare at stake, and only two of them, so it is essential to maintain things as they are to facilitate continued growth and recovery.

These are words here, not deeds, which is the difference between my parents and myself. And I have earned the right to write them.

I respect the fact that my siblings may be on different stages of their recovery, and may choose to protect themselves with denial as I did in the past. I hope we can become more united as time goes on, but I am now 52 years old and am finished with merely surviving! I CHOOSE to THRIVE!

It is so easy to think, "why am I such a bad person that I can't live up to these expectations?" Whereas what was asked of me was impossible and unreasonable, it wasn't humanly possible to deliver on those expectations. In plain and simple terms it was manipulation using a double standard.

As Mark Twain said about himself, I too have a "sleepy conscience." It all boils down to having a conscience. Some people do, and some people don't, and conscience is on a continuum. I am not annoying myself about how they feel because it is probable that their denial and self-pity will keep them insulated anyway.

It takes us a while sometimes, to put it together, especially when we've grown up in that kind of environment, and that's all we've known, you know? When abuse begins when we are very young we don't have a good frame of reference to know how to begin life as an adult. At our core we know that there's something better, there's has to be something much better, but we don't have a frame of reference.

Anger is bad for you. The other thing I would say is to grow at your own pace. Because we have been programmed wrong, we are going to make mistakes. Small mistakes. We can learn from those small mistakes and move on. Our frame of reference can be developed. It's not a finite thing from one day to the other. It's something that we're acquiring and that we're working on as time goes on.

Staying safe is your priority. Give back and support others. For me, that means walking away and moving on. I see no alternative. It is imperative to find a support group of strangers to support you.

There is this "fractured family syndrome," that arises from an abusive home. Your own emotions and those of your nearest and dearest are too volatile and fragile to deal with it within the family circle (in the beginning anyway, this can change as time goes by). Love yourself enough to do what it takes to heal.

I Am Worth It!

By Mirelle Wright

*M*y story of abuse started at a very young age, I believe around the age of three or four. In my life, most of the male figures in my life put me down and called me hurtful names. As a preteen and teenager, I looked older for my age and men would make passes and sexual advances towards me.

Feelings and beliefs of not being worthy, not being lovable, feeling disgusting, feeling like a nuisance to everyone became my foundation of what was to come later in life. These feelings kept me in survival mode to where the feelings of shame, detachment, depression, and abandonment were common for me. I turned to bulimia and anorexia as a coping mechanism. I was in many dead-end relationships and was promiscuous in hopes to feel loved and safe.

When I met my ex-husband, I felt all of this was behind me now. We dated for about a year and a half before getting married. I was content in my marriage. I had three wonderful stepchildren, a supportive husband, and a great career. One day, all of that crashing down, the day I found out my husband cheated on me. Devastated, I had no idea how to cope with this loss and grief. The one person I trusted wouldn't abandon me just did so.

We separated for two months until I found out my stepdaughter was pregnant at 16. We discussed and agreed to try to make our marriage work;

however, it was, unfortunately, a lost cause. Almost three months later, I experienced trauma I would never have thought possible to experience.

As a 911 dispatcher for 14 years, I dealt with domestic violence victims on a regular basis. Never did I ever think I would become one. One night, my ex-husband had too much to drink. We were arguing, which we never did during our marriage, and I tried to go past him. He pushed me into the wall where my head hit the corner of the window sill causing me to go completely black. Finally, things started to come into focus as I lay on the floor. I looked up and saw a look on his face I had never seen before. The more things came into focus; I saw that he had a shotgun. To this day, I cannot remember if the gun was pointed at me or not

As I lay there, he looked down with a look of fear and regret of what had just happened. He had never been violent or abusive to me before. At that time, he left the house, and I called the police; the people I worked with to make the report about my assault. After reporting to the police, I was taken to the hospital and advised I had a concussion. The doctor questioned me about what happened, but I could not tell him the truth because of the embarrassment and shame. I did not tell him I had been pushed by someone, that I tripped and ran into the window sill.

Eventually, I lost my job as a dispatcher due to not being able to cope with what had happened. I believe I that's when I first had to deal with my PTSD. What made it worse is I felt victimized by my coworkers. They, like everyone, felt I should just "get over it." My coworkers were supposed to be this "Law Enforcement Family," but they too turned their backs on me. It was because I couldn't cope, and they did not have the information on how to help someone that experienced trauma. They only dealt with crisis management. I didn't have any skills to deal with the abandonment and trauma. I felt lost and alone with no identity. My identity was being his wife and a 911 dispatcher.

I went into a dark period for almost a year. I felt like there was no way out, that I was always to feel that way. The emotional pain was so overwhelming that I just didn't want to "be here anymore." It's not that I wanted to die, I just wanted the pain to stop. I had taken a handful of pills. I called my best friend, and he ended up coming over. If it were not for him, I would not be here today. He found me almost unconscious, so he called for an ambulance.

Due to my health and emotional state, my mom and step-dad talked me into moving to Arizona from Oregon, which ended up being the best thing to happen to me. I realized I suffered from PTSD, and thought I had it under control. I went back to school, gained confidence, met amazing new people. I finally was discovering who I was and what Mirelle liked.

I graduated with my bachelor's degree and got a job in the field of study. During that time, I met my ex-boyfriend. He turned my life upside down in less than a year. I felt like I was going crazy. I would cry uncontrollably every night, not eat, could not concentrate, hyper-aroused, and shut out my family and friends.

My breaking point was when I ended up in the hospital and didn't remember why. The first thing I remember was waking up, and discovering that I was being restrained. Due to my PTSD, I went into a panic attack, so they sedated me. When I finally saw the social worker, she told me I had ecstasy in my system. There was no way! I had never done an illegal drug in my life. My ex-boyfriend was the only one I was around that night, and he had made me a drink. I would have never thought he would drug me. I finally realized I needed to leave. I could no longer take the emotional and sexual abuse from him and was afraid for my life after that.

This time I absolutely could not snap out of my PTSD darkness. I dealt with an abusive relationship and was dealing with an abusive supervisor at work. This is something I have not shared publicly until now, and what pushed me over the edge was being diagnosed with HSV1 & HSV2 (both herpes simplex viruses) in which my ex-boyfriend knew he had, and never shared with me. I felt disgusting. Who would ever want me now? It was a constant reminder for months after I left due to the stress and anxiety causing breakouts for almost four months straight. I slipped into a major depressive state, stuck in an excruciating PTSD episode, and started to isolate. The depression was worse than I had ever experienced! I felt like my life had no purpose, and that I was weak, disgusting, and had got myself into "another abusive relationship" that was way worse than before. I reached a point to where I didn't want to live anymore. I had never been in this state of mind before. I felt like a burden, a failure, crazy, and weak. Why even go on living?

I was blessed things had finally changed. During my journey, I found it almost impossible to get the mental health help that I so desperately needed. It seemed like nobody wanted to help or you had to wait six months to get a counselor. Thankfully, I continued to push forward and finally got the help I needed that has helped me with coping, recognizing the triggers, and how to work through those triggers. I still suffer from sleeplessness and nightmares; however, it has gotten better.

My journey has not been easy. At times, it was downright painful and put me in an extremely dark place. With educating myself and the different therapies I have been through, my passion and mission in life are in sexual and domestic violence/abuse advocacy and awareness. My motto is to "never to let anyone feel alone in their struggle." I want men and women to know that there is life after abuse no matter what the case (abuse is not gendered specific). I know what it's like to feel alone in a life surrounded by darkness, humiliation, shame, and the desire to not live anymore. I want to tell my complete story with the hope that it gives others the courage to find peace and love that they deserve, both men and women survivors of abuse.

Two of the most positive things I have done for myself to overcome my trauma is fighting for the therapy I deserved and helping other victims/survivors. I finally found someone that listened and helped guide me to the freedom I have never felt before. I was blessed and assertive enough to fight for what I needed and deserved to deal with the decades of abuse I had endured. I have completed DBT (Dialectal Behavioral Therapy), individual trauma work, and some EMDR (Eye Movement Desensitization and Reprocessing). I am always educating myself on sexual and domestic abuse/violence.

What I have found has helped me the most is helping others. Feeling alone to where I felt nobody understood what I was going through and feeling like a burden to those people, I help others through that trauma and into a journey of healing by just being a listening ear. Being in the process of organizing support groups, workshops and speaking engagements, I am hoping to reach those who feel there is no way out.

The best thing to do is get help! Do not settle for anything less than what you deserve. Fight for your therapy so you can learn to love yourself. Try DBT therapy, as it can help you fight demons you have been fighting for years, and give you some peace. Triggers will still rear their ugly heads, but you will have the tools and support to deal with them. DBT helped me to cope with the PTSD symptoms such as nightmares, anxiety, and hyper-vigilance, just to name a few. DON'T be afraid to tell your story!

Educate yourself as much as possible. People believe the most difficult step is getting out of the abuse. Although it is one of the most difficult, I found trying to figure out my life after leaving to be the hardest. You're discovering you don't know what you like, who you are, how to deal with all of the overwhelming feelings, and so many more personal feelings you may have never had to deal with before. You're trying to figure out how to love yourself and find out what you like and don't like because you've been suppressed. You haven't been able to be you. Someone took that ability from you, and it's overwhelming to get it back. Research the feeling you are experiencing because it will help you understand how to help yourself. It is a slow, painful journey that is well worth the effort.

Some of the resources that helped me in my journey are DBT, EMDR, and individualized trauma therapy! I also recommend a book that I read that helped me realize how much emotional abuse I had been through and how detrimental it was to my declining health. The book is, "The Verbally Abusive Relationship: How to Recognize It, and How to Respond," by Patricia Evans. It goes through many scenarios in which I experienced during the time with my ex-boyfriend.

In my journey, I discovered I am worth it, I love not being I survival mode all of the time, and most of all I can make a difference. And I will make a difference!

Mirelle Wright

As a survivor of domestic violence, sexual abuse, and a woman all too familiar with Post Traumatic Stress Disorder, Mirelle Wright is a successful and passionate advocate of Domestic Violence Awareness and Intervention, for both men and women. As the Founder of Mirelle Wright Coaching, she takes the hearts and minds of individuals and transforms their old patterns of thinking into success. She knows and understands the past, has the power to affect your present and future, and is determined to help others overcome their own blocks.

Mirelle is living proof that no one is their past nor are they what happened to them. While overcoming multiple obstacles from restraining orders to court hearings, she found the time at the age of 38 to make a better life for herself. Mirelle successfully graduated with honors and made the Dean's List with her bachelor's degree from Arizona State University in Nonprofit Leadership and Management.

Despite her past, Mirelle knows that no matter your circumstances, life is to be fully lived. Everyone must stand up for themselves with confidence and command their dreams. Life should never be feared nor be limited by the power of others.

Mirelle's Video Interview: **https://youtu.be/KaK7zDZGEgI**

It's Not Your Fault!

By Rhiannon Smith

I grew up with an alcoholic father who was physically and emotionally abusive to myself, my siblings, and my mother. There was one instance where I was beaten with a wooden fish filet board so badly that I couldn't go to school for a couple of days because the bruises on my legs and thighs were too visible.

The abusiveness from my father came to a head when I was 14, when I witnessed him assault, and shoot my soon-to-be stepfather.

Aside from my dad, I was molested by my best friend's stepfather when I was 12. I didn't tell anyone until I was an adult. It was just such a chaotic time of my life when I didn't realize that what was happening to me was wrong.

I would say that right now; I am probably at my healthiest self in all areas of my life. Healing from a past of abuse has been a choice and a journey. I have finally made peace with my ghosts, and yet, I acknowledge they will never fully go away.

As part of my healing journey, I volunteered for MOCSA, which is a nonprofit organization that helps both women and men that are survivors of sexual trauma.

I also worked at a domestic violence shelter for about a year, and that was cathartic as well. Outside of social work, I went through some intensive therapy, specifically EMDR, or "Eye Movement Desensitization and Reprocessing." It is a psychotherapy treatment that was designed to alleviate the distress associated with traumatic memories.

Cindy Wilson at Scottsdale, AZ Psychological, helped me to change my life. Having been diagnosed with PTSD with symptoms that were often debilitating, she helped me to get my life back.

I also began yoga and guided meditation practice that I go to a few times a week at Anahata Yoga. I have also found sound healing to be extremely helpful.

For those who are just awakening to the knowingness that it is time to begin their healing journey, I would say first and foremost, that what you went through was not your fault. Shame is such an unfortunate component of surviving abuse. It sounds so cliché, but you must come to realize that you are so much stronger than you think you are, and you do have the power to yourself to heal and change your life. That power comes from the goodness that is deep within you.

I hope that you will tap into whatever resources that resonate with you to get help. You do not have to take this journey alone.

Rhiannon Smith

Rhiannon grew up in Northwest Missouri, traveling and living all over North America before settling in the West. She has a degree in Business Administration with a focus in Marketing.

Rhiannon has spent a large portion of her adult years working on her degree and studying human interactions. This has helped her express her humor and adventures through writing. She lives in Scottsdale with her two cats Ray-Ray and Baby Cat, whom she wrote her first children's book about and became a Bestselling Author.

The Adventures of Rizzie Muffin Monster: **http://amzn.to/2HHq9h8**

Rhiannon's Video Interview: **https://youtu.be/ReXWjqKJ3SU**

"Our deepest fear is not that we
are inadequate. Our deepest fear
is that we are powerful beyond
measure. It is our light...
not our darkness that
frightens us most."

Marianne Williamson

Beware of Re-Victimization

By Winnie Anderson

*W*hat I'm about to share is my story.

You may see elements of yourself and your story in my journey, but I wanted to join this movement and share what I went through and am going through because I want to help others who are still early in their healing journey.

I want to help people–especially women–realize they don't have to be trapped by the past.

I think my suffering was necessary to make me the person I am, but I also believe I had to develop the strength to help others come out of the other side of this. I think it's my calling to help others embrace the positive gifts they developed as a result of their experiences and to recognize that they're not chained by the past.

It might not seem like there's anything positive about what happened, but I believe it's up to us to find or to create something positive from it.

I know first-hand how our abuse experience can cause deep scars that eventually can lead to our holding ourselves back from achieving the success we dream of and deserve.

I want to help people break out of that dis-empowering pattern, and I feel one way to do that is to tell my story.

My abuse started before I was even born.

My mother regularly told my siblings and me that she didn't want us, that she was sorry she had ever gotten pregnant, and that she never wanted to have any children.

I think she had a lot of anger around being a woman in the period she lived in and felt resentful that as a Roman Catholic wife in the 1950s–she had no options but to have sex and risk getting pregnant.

As a 54-year old woman, I can understand that she didn't want children and I believe getting pregnant should be a conscious choice for a woman. So I understand the point that my mom was making, but I don't excuse her for what she said and how she said it to us. She was the adult and should have had better control over her emotions.

Instead, I believe her anger, resentment, and self-loathing, as well as hatred towards her unborn child, was absorbed by me. I wrestled with self-hatred myself decades.

I think the abuse officially started right after I was born since I don't have any memories of being held or hugged or shown any affection by my mother.

My earliest memories are of her calling me awful names, telling me I was ugly, stupid, and that I'd never amount to anything.

I never thought of what was happening as abuse. I just thought that she was incredibly mean. In my early 20's I finally came to terms with what happened and recognized that what I had experienced was abuse.

I felt calling it that was enough. I believed I survived and that was it.

But of course, it wasn't. I think my greatest obstacle to getting past the abuse was being re-victimized without realizing what was going on.

I worked for abusive bosses and had abusive friendships. I had poor boundaries that caused me to over-deliver for clients to the point that there was no way I could be profitable in my work.

But I also struggled with being re-victimized by my mother.

One of the biggest issues for me that contributed to my allowing myself to be re-victimized is I have a sister who lives with my mom. My other sister lives nearby.

As much as I don't care about my mother, I don't want to lose my relationships with my siblings. So I would go home to visit – back into the lion's den if you will – to visit my sisters and I'm committed to doing what it takes to maintain our relationships.

I did realize that while I was deep in recovery and while I was in therapy there was just no way I could go home. I had to protect myself first. I took several months off from visiting.

I told my oldest sister and my younger brother why I wasn't going home, but I couldn't bring myself to discuss it with the sister who still lived at home. I felt bad about that. I lied to my sister. But we all make the best decisions and choices we can at the moment, and that was the best I could do.

I knew that once I left after a visit, my sister would get an increased level of her abuse and I didn't want to contribute to that. I So my focus was on protecting myself, but also protecting my relationship with my sister.

Another challenge to getting past the abuse was people–who I'm sure meant well–telling me to get over it. People like my husband and some friends.

Of course, I knew I had to get over it, but I also knew I had to process what happened and each of us has to do that at our own pace.

I think the biggest aha moment for me in my healing was hitting 50. One of the great gifts of aging is becoming comfortable with who we are, and for many of us, it's also deciding to take back control of our lives.

I recognized my mother had stolen the first half of my life and I could continue to allow that and let her take the rest of my life, or I could say "Enough."

On the one hand, I had tried to be the bigger person and think "I'm not going to be triggered by her. I'm not going to get sucked in."

But at the same time, I realized I had to stand up for myself. There was and is only so much I can do out of concern for my relationship with my sisters. I had to accept that it's not selfish to protect myself.

I decided that if it meant telling my mom to shut up, or telling her that I was leaving because I wasn't going to sit there and listen to her crap anymore, then that's what I was going to do. And that's what I did.

Success gurus talk about the importance of taking responsibility for your thoughts and actions, but what I had to accept responsibility for was that I'm not responsible for others.

I'm only responsible for what I can control. I can't control when she was going to snap and come out with some vicious statement, but I can control whether I absorb that and whether I stand up for and protect myself.

If you're just starting this journey, prepare yourself because it's going to be painful. But I promise it's worth it. You deserve to be treated with kindness and respect.

Get support. Find a way to gather strength from others who are going through it or who have gone through it. It's a never-ending journey of continued growth and healing.

I equate it to the recovery process alcoholics go through. Recovering from alcoholism is a day to day recovery process in staying healthy. I think it's also important to understand how you learn and process information best and to be kind to yourself.

One of my escapes as a child was reading. I could be completely quiet and escape into the story. So my first reaction, whenever I have a problem, is there must be a book that has an answer for me.

The book that helped me the most was amazing workbook called "Survivor to Thriver." The workbook, offered as a free download, was created by the Morris Center, and the website is **www.acasupport.org**.

That book helped educate me about the impact of what happened to me and helped me to recognize the dis-empowering patterns I'd developed and then to begin the work to let go of them.

Brené Brown and her TEDx talk, as well as her appearance on Oprah's Super Soul Sunday, were incredibly powerful for me. I then read all of her books.

I also read specific books on behavior patterns resulting from abuse and those were written by Beverly Engel.

I found her books so powerful that I reached out to her and worked privately with her.

I also think it's important to recognize that your abuse is your abuse. There's no comparing your experience to someone else and thinking you shouldn't feel bad, because it could have been worse, and we don't judge someone else thinking that they shouldn't feel bad because what they went through wasn't as bad as what others have gone through.

Abuse is abuse, and it's all awful.

Winnie Anderson

Winnie Anderson is a Business and Achievement Coach for introverted entrepreneurs. She helps coaches, consultants, healers, and creatives break free from dis-empowering patterns and beliefs and break through to achieve their goals with courage, confidence, clarity, and compassion.

Winnie was knocked out of the traditional workforce and her position as Director of HR for a nonprofit as a result of injuries sustained in a car accident in 1999.

She reinvented herself and became an award-winning brand strategist and copywriter.

While working to recover from her Traumatic Brain Injury, Winnie recognized that the beliefs and behavior patterns she developed to survive an abusive home life growing up were actively holding her back as an independent professional.

She struggled with fear of rejection, an inability to set and hold boundaries with clients, perfectionism, and dismally low self-esteem.

As she began to heal from her emotional trauma, she recognized similar patterns and beliefs at work in her clients and potential clients. They often struggled to stand out while not really wanting to stand out. They also dealt with fears of success and fears of failure.

Their beliefs and patterns kept them stuck and struggling to move forward to create the lives and achieve the success they wanted.

As Winnie healed herself and began to achieve her own goals – of becoming a best-selling author, producing a popular podcast, and building a brand that would attract opportunities and people who were pre-sold on working with her – she began telling her story and reshaping her business to help others.

Learn more about her and discover how courageous an entrepreneur you are by visiting her website at **WinnieAnderson.com**

Social media links
Facebook business page:
https://www.facebook.com/courageousentrepreneurshow/
Facebook personal page: http://facebook.com/winnie.anderson1
Twitter: http://twitter.com/winnie_anderson
YouTube:
https://www.youtube.com/channel/UCrPYOY1GV7GGr7G3ug9EWA
LinkedIn: http://linkedin.com/in/winnieanderson
Video Interview: https://youtu.be/vISE8X5lAqE

"Create the highest, grandest
vision possible for your life, because
you become what you believe."

Oprah Winfrey

We Came Full Circle

By Oshikan Sjodin-Bunse

Scene 586:

Sister: "Would you like cake or pie for your birthday?"

Me: "Pumpkin pie! I love it and can't buy in Germany."

Sister: "What kind? The store carries pumpkin mixed with cheesecake, caramel or chocolate."

Me: "Really? Pumpkin pie sure has changed!"

Mother: "If you don't decide which type of pie you want, I'm going to smear it in your face!"

Feelings of fun about celebrating my birthday with family and my dear friend, who had traveled with me from Germany to California, jarringly disappeared.-Age 43.

Scene 421:

Me: "How do you like my t-shirt that I silk-screened Grandma's old dinner plate design onto?"

Mother: "Take off that disgusting hippie top that you can see your boobs through or I'm going to take these scissors and cut it off of you! You're such a whore!"

I ran outside to escape my mother chasing me with scissors because I knew she would not carry through with trying to cut my t-shirt off of me in front of our neighbors.- Age 16.

An Early Scene:
Me: Standing in front of a visitor and proudly lifting my dress to show my pretty new underpants.
Mother: "Put your dress down right now! Bad girl! Shame on you! Shame on you! Bad girl!"– Age 2 or 3.

And so shamed I was, that I still remember the scene and my feelings - at age 60.

*W*elcome to my former world of psychological, emotional, verbal and a bit of physical abuse. The scenes above are but a mere snippet of the myriad episodes of crazy-making and aggressive behavior that I experienced with my mother.

The Pain of It All
"Sticks and stones will break my bones, but words can never hurt me." What a ridiculous children's rhyme! Who were we trying to convince when we chanted this to the mean word slingers? I surely did not dare to utter this chant out loud as I tried to protect myself from my mother's onslaught of angry and ugly words, but I remember saying it silently. I also dared not raise my fists to my chest in an attempt to ward off her barbed words from reaching my heart, but I pretended that I did. These childish self-protective imaginings did not save me from the effects of her attacks. The chant was useless and the barbs my mother shot were aimed expertly to slip through my make-believe upraised fists, to pierce my heart with precision.

It's over now. My mother is dead. I will never again hear words from her that informed me in some way, shape, or form that, "I'm just no good." Or will I? Her main message to me still spooks around in my head, but now thank goodness, much more rarely.

In a perfect world, our caretakers are the ones to cherish and strengthen us in the knowledge that we are worthy of love and respect. If instead, we are emotionally abused or neglected by the very mother, father or primary caretaker that is supposed to protect us, the consequences are grave, even if the weapons used are words and not a raised fist or an assault on our private parts.

Children don't have the vocabulary or psychological understanding (heck, we rarely have it as adults) to comprehend the tactics of an abusive person. Kids have not yet learned how to protect themselves from abusive harm, though some are born with strong resilience.

As a child and teen, I often knew that the way my mother treated me was wrong. I had this recognition, but I was helpless to change the situation. My teenage years were the hardest, both for my mother and for me. My father was ill, my mother's mother lamed, my brother was suffering from Schizophrenia. My mother told me she felt like she was pedaling a five-seat bike with the sick family members sitting passively behind her. In her mind, I jumped on too for a free ride and burdened her even more with my wayward ways. Her voice was full of hate and scorn that I caused her even more trouble. I felt sad about her heavy load and angry and hurt that she had such a negative opinion of me.

I was ridiculed, manipulated, verbally abused and subjected to psychological and emotional warfare by my mother. I was also physically well cared for, and there were decidedly good times in my family. I was driven to cheer-leading practice, art classes, modeling school and sometimes lovingly, if not a bit aggressively, tickled by my mother. This double bind, of being pulled in and then pushed away, is what made for so much confusion in my heart and head. 'It's complicated,' is a very succinct way to describe the feelings I had for my mother.

When I stopped modeling school and became a California hippie of the 70's, I also morphed into a non-compliant and rebellious daughter. This increased the wrathful barbs shot in my direction exponentially. I had sex with my boyfriend, Bob. After my mother discovered birth control in my room, he was never greeted or spoken to for five years. My mother's favorite description for me, 'whore' was used incessantly. I was coerced to sign a contract, stating that I had to stop seeing my friends and boyfriend, not have sex until I was married and throw away my hippie clothes, or be thrown out. I signed but did none of the above. I did run away a couple of times, she locked me out a couple more, I was threatened with loss of my home, but I was never actually thrown out of the house.

My willingness to let off steam and articulate my frustration helped me not to bury these 'over the top' dramas in the dark recesses of my mind. I did not suppress my experiences, and I am convinced that being able to articulate what went down, kept me sane. I will be forever grateful to my oldest friends who listened so compassionately to my ranting and drama stories. These friendships have lasted to this day as we feel a deep sense of belonging, protectiveness, and love for one another.

In her excellent book, "Difficult Mothers," Terri Apter has created a clear definition of the difference between a 'good enough' parent and a difficult parent. She writes, "All parents have ups and downs. All parents have bad days. A few bouts of anger, a smattering of unreasonable demands, occasional neediness, a careless or vicious word, do not make a difficult mother. In a significant psychological sense, a difficult mother is a great deal more than a mother who is sometimes difficult. Though difficult mothers come in many different guises, there is an underlying pattern. A difficult mother is one who presents her child with the dilemma: "Either develop complex and constricting coping mechanisms to maintain a relationship with me, at great cost to your own outlook, imagination, and values, or suffer ridicule, disapproval, or rejection."

She goes on further to explain, "A child cannot easily escape this dilemma. A child does not have the option to say, "I don't care whether you think I'm bad" or "I don't care whether you notice me" or "I don't care whether you are angry or disapproving." A child is terrified at the prospect of being abandoned. The primitive panic at abandonment lasts long after the physical helplessness of the infant ends. Even as adults, we are rarely willing to renounce a mother's love even when it brings pain, frustration, and disappointment."

My sense of right, wrong and what is fair, my open disregard and disobedience of my mother's values and rules, still could not keep me from developing a very negative internal criticism system. I was outwardly a rebel but actually a very good girl. I drank the poison. I did what she taught me and continued with the harsh chastising of myself.

As time went on, my mother's transmitted root message of, "You're no good!" nestled itself ever deeper into my psyche, but with more complicated twists. My internal and infernal messages became, "I just can't do it!" "I dare not go public with my eclectic ways, or I will be ridiculed." "I just don't have it in me to be successful." "No one really loves me."

Change Is In The Air
It turns out that these messages are a bunch of crock! I have learned to change these automatic go-to thoughts into much kinder beliefs about myself. And some pretty cool people love me, as I do them. I have transformed the fearful and frustrated part of me into someone who is passionate and confident enough to share the knowledge I have gained. I have dared to 'come out' and be my eclectic self.

You too may have an emotionally immature mother. She may not have been the vengeful type as mine was, but since you are reading this book, my guess is that you, or someone you know, have experienced abuse.

This chapter is not only a portrayal of what emotional and psychological abuse can look like. No! Comprehending what this rather hidden type of abuse encompasses, is only the first step to living a life where self-love, self-worth, and self-trust become natural ways of being for thriver's once again.

The title of this book proclaims, "We Choose to Thrive" and I write in the hope that you will be inspired to try what I have found to be effective ways to recover from abuse. It doesn't matter whether your abuse was verbal, sexual, or physical beatings; all abuse messes with our heads and our hearts.

Survivors of abuse are left to deal with no longer believing in how wonderful they actually are. We often experience guilt, shame and a lack of trust - both in ourselves and in others. We are bewildered that someone who is supposed to love us is being so hurtful. There is rage, lack of an ability to set healthy boundaries, staying lost in victim-hood and the fear that we will repeat the same behavior with our loved ones. This is a lot to bounce back and change the effects of, but it certainly can be done!

Though it has been a long and winding road, I have figured out how to free myself from the after-effects of the abuse listed above. Along my journey, I've discovered great tools and mindsets that I now share with other wayfarers. These are three of the most important areas of transformation I concentrate on:

1) Replace unkind internalized beliefs with a newfound love trust and respect for the beautiful being that you are.

2) Change harmful maternal behavior for the sake of the innocents in our charge; our children.

3) Learn if and how your relationship with your mother is salvageable.

My Bounce-back Journey
My youngest daughter once made a rough estimate that I have at least a few thousand dollars and euros worth of psychology and self-help books on my shelves. It's true as I've been reading psychology books 'for fun' since high school. The first book that I simply could not put down about the mother-daughter relationship is Victoria Secunda's, "When You and Your Mother Can't Be Friends: Resolving the Most Complicated Relationship of Your Life." This book portrays different types of controlling mothers and the reactions that daughters form in response.

Victoria Secunda also describes what kind of relationship might be possible with your mother. She details what it would entail to become friends, or if that is not possible, to at least reach a truce. Some adult children find it necessary to 'divorce' and have no contact with their mothers when she is so damaged that the only way to retain their own safety and sanity is to terminate the relationship with her.

This book gave me the confidence to suggest to my mom that we go to therapy together. I was willing to leave my kids and husband in Germany and move back to California for a while to do this. This is how much I wanted to improve our relationship. She said that she did not want to revisit the past or have therapy. It was then that I decided to go the no contact route for a while and distance myself from so much turbulence. I saw this as a way to regain my own sense of self as separate from her tirade of disparaging remarks.

For the next three years, I sent birthday and Christmas cards, but there were no phone calls or visits during that time. I could not bring myself to send her Mother's Day cards. Our suspended relationship helped me to see much more clearly the effect her abuse had on me. I started to feel freer and stronger, and I enjoyed my life much more.

I knew that I eventually wanted to re-connect with my mother. I felt that if we never spoke or saw each other again, we would for sure be bringing our unresolved karma into another lifetime. That is the last thing I wanted to do! I felt strongly that even if she was not interested in change, I wanted some type of resolution and peace for myself. For me, this included having some contact.

It was during this pause from my mother that I began pursuing my long-time interest in psychology and became a Heilpraktiker fuer Psychotherapie < German, (Healing Practitioner for Psychotherapy). With my newfound knowledge, I unofficially diagnosed my mother as having Narcissistic Personality Disorder, NPD. Her obsession with victimization, her bullying, and fiercely unapologetic ways fit perfectly to NPD. Gaining a good grasp of my mother's psychology helped me understand why she was so manipulative and into blame shifting.

It was also helpful to speak with a family member who knew my mother as a child and learn that my grandmother also had emotionally and psychologically abused my mother. I knew my maternal grandmother to be a very difficult and sarcastic person, so this was easy to imagine. I had an 'Aha' moment concerning the negative family legacy that had been passed down through the generations when, in the heat of blaming me for my 'awful' behavior, she shouted that she hated her mother but had never, ever spoken back to her mother as I did to her!

Here was the crux of the matter! Influenced by the time and culture of her generation, plus by her own decision, my mother never took the chance to examine why she was so angry and why she acted out so vehemently towards others. She told me that she never expressed disagreement with her mother and made it clear to me that this was a very bad thing to do. I can surmise that her hurt festered within and would make her periodically explode. With this realization, the shackles of confusion about our messy relationship started to loosen. I strongly advocate that people self-reflect and put in the effort to recover from a problematic childhood, so they do not pass on negative family patterns!

The Good Stuff
As I mentioned above, learning what constitutes emotional and psychological abuse to understand the type of controlling behavior that you have been subjected to, is only part of the journey to recovery.

What I've found to be extremely effective and beneficial, both for my clients and myself is to practice research-based exercises from the Applied Science of Positive Psychology and to meditate.

After studying the half-empty glass of all that can go emotionally and psychologically wrong with us, I felt the need to take a good look at the half-full glass on what can help us to flourish and be happy. Thus began my studies and continued excitement for the ever-evolving findings from the field of Positive Psychology.

Positive Psychology contains the study of what is right and good about us. In my first course, our beginning homework exercise was to introduce ourselves with a concrete story that showed us acting at our best. We were instructed to remember a story that illustrated our highest strength. At a later time, I did this exercise with a classroom of fourteen-year-olds. First, I introduced the concept that we all have top Character Strengths and that our happiness levels are higher when we concentrate on our natural strengths instead of what we consider to be our flaws and weaknesses. I gave them a detailed list of the 24 strengths that have been researched to show up pretty consistently in almost all cultures the world over.

Once the teens got over their conditioned response of believing that expressing a personal story about something positive smacked of boasting, they learned amazing things about each other. As the students listened to each other, they kept a lookout for the positives and guessed which strengths were in use by their classmates. Their teacher expressed to me later that this simple exercise created a sense of deepened respect for each other.

Here are the steps to this simple writing exercise to try if you would like a quick boost in how you feel about yourself.

First, visit the website:

https://www.authentichappiness.sas.upenn.edu,

Go to Questionnaires, login and take the free VIA Survey of Character Strengths.

After answering the questions, you will receive a list with your top strengths.

You can then contemplate with more understanding which top strength you were using in the experience you will write about and integrate it into your story.

It was quite emotional for me to see my Character Strengths printed in black and white. There was a sense of, "Yes, this is me! These are characteristics that are important to me, and they reflect a good part of who I am!"

Best Self Exercise:

Write a roughly 300-word concrete story that shows you at your best and illustrates your highest strength. The story should have a beginning, middle, and end with a bang, not a whimper. Discovering your Character Strengths and writing a truly positive story about when you were at your best, is a good start to healing the cracks in your self-love, self-worth, and self-trust. Share your story with someone you trust. Appreciate which combination of strengths is uniquely you and begin to use them in ever new and unusual ways.

I loved what I was learning in my studies but had an unexpected shock when Martin Seligman, father of the Positive Psychology movement and my main teacher, declared a rather revolutionary idea in the field of psychology. Through his research into learned helplessness and learned optimism, he discovered that we do not have to rehash over and over our painful childhood memories to be able to thrive in our lives.

At first, I was in total disagreement! I had spent two years lying on a therapist's couch, recalling and describing in minute detail all the ugly scenes and dramas of my youth and beyond. After hearing my respected teacher's proclamation, I took a closer look at my experience with therapy and realized that the only thing that had really come of it was that I was sure it was my mother and not me who was crazier on the crazy scale. I also realized that the positive psychology exercises that I was now doing had me feeling a whole lot better, a whole lot quicker than the two years of telling my seemingly endless chronicle of sad and frustrating tales to my therapist. Martin Seligman had a point!

I now know that it does not take years of rehashing what went on in the past to live a flourishing life. Knowledge of what went down and how it has affected you is important to know, but only up to a point. Most important is what we do with our lives now.

Caveat: If there is suppression of memory or if you feel overwhelmed, then it might be a good idea to be gently guided in remembering what happened to you and integrate your past with your life now. Speak with a trauma expert if this is you.

I continued practicing my training exercises that have been specifically designed to increase pleasure, engagement, and meaning in people's lives. Learning how to create a greater depth of meaning and a sense of accomplishment is also important pillars of Positive Psychology. There are exercises that can be used to build better relationships. Without my mother aware of what I was doing when I called or visited, the exercises and mindset that I practiced helped create a higher ratio of pleasant emotion between us. Take that in, please. I could better our relationship and my feelings towards her, without her changing at all!

The next big healing modality that I want to mention is meditation. While my husband, kids and I were living in Japan, I was trained to teach Metta

Bhavana or Loving Kindness meditation. In this meditation, you first give yourself the gift of loving energy in whatever form is needed by you at the moment. You then imagine different people - a friend, a neutral person and a person you are having difficulties with -and give them all the gift of loving-kindness.

This is a very transformative meditation that begins with you first. As we know, the more you love yourself, the easier it is to love others. It can bring up strong resistance to gift your enemy with loving kindness, but if you persevere it will get easier, and you will feel much lighter over time. My mother was often in the seat of honor of the difficult person, and this meditation helped me release my hateful feelings towards her.

Another very powerful meditation is called, "Feeding Your Demons." There is a book by the same name that explains the concept in detail. In this meditation, you give form to something that is bothering you and then ask this 'demon' questions about what it wants and needs and how it will feel once you give it what it asks for. You listen to the demon's answers and proceed to feed it your most precious possession, your body. You imagine that your body has dissolved into nectar. When the demon has drunk and is fully satisfied, it changes form or disappears. You then get to hear a beautiful message from an ally and rest in the inevitable peacefulness that has appeared. I am amazed every time I do this meditation at the insights and the comfort that I receive!

I cannot do these two meditations justice with only a paragraph dedicated to each, but I mention them in the hope that you will explore further how they work, the beneficial results and even the positive brain changes that come from having a regular meditation practice.

The mindset and practices that I have learned from positive psychology and meditation help me better address whatever I may currently find challenging in my life. Meditation helps me transcend unhelpful emotions. Meditation and the exercises that I do affect me at a deep level to feel secure in my decision to go after what I am called to do. Meditation is a direct line to my inner wisdom and, if you will, my spirit guides.

What else has been helpful to live a flourishing life?

Taking to heart that whatever I focus on grows, it is always good to remember to pay more attention to the beautiful and good things in life as our brains are wired to experience negatives in a stronger way. This is our survival instinct. I do not ignore problems, but I use my healthier mindset and practices to steer me away from wallowing and ruminating. I prefer to ask myself how I can overcome a challenge and to even go so far as to be grateful for what may overwhelm or scare me. I know that once I take necessary steps, I will be proud of what I have accomplished. I appreciate my strength of grit and perseverance.

When I am stressed, I must be careful not to slip into the old pattern of harshly chastising myself. People who have been abused have to be vigilant to ensure that the new synapses they have formed in their brains that inform a more positive way of seeing themselves, continue to grow and become thick and strong. With this, the more positive ways of thinking become the first or at least the second go-to thoughts.

Victims of abuse, now thriver's, must consciously choose to ignore old destructive messages and be extra kind and gentle with themselves. The downward thinking and feeling spiral becomes weaker the more you concentrate on what is cool and beautiful about you. I'm not speaking about narcissism or false pride. I'm talking about loving yourself, knowing your strengths and appreciating how resilient you are. It is a practice with great rewards. Speak to yourself as a good friend does.

'Soft structures' are what I like to call boundaries and setting them with my mother also helped. When we saw each other again after the three-year break, I told her that I would not stay with her but rather with my sister and friends. I left the room or house when she was abusive, and I kept reminding myself that her words had nothing to do with me and everything to do with her own unexamined psychology.

Compassion and forgiveness are also good antidotes to the poison of abusive behavior, but they must not be taken prematurely. Compassion arose when I better understood how damaged my mother was, and how difficult her life had been. I do not advocate 'forgive and forget' since that often cannot be sustained. An exercise that helped me begin forgiving my mother was writing her a forgiveness letter. I didn't send this letter, and do not recommend doing so, but it helped me to let go of a lot of the aversion I had felt for so long. If forgiveness is just too much for you to consider, then writing a letter of 'letting go' may be more beneficial to you.

Gratitude is another great practice. You may be familiar with writing a Gratitude Journal. It has been rigorously proven through various studies that just one week of writing down three good things that happened to you, and what you had to do to make them happen, will increase your happiness levels even six months down the road!

I'm not advocating being grateful about your abusive experiences, but for the things big and small, that are good in your life right now. When you shift your perception to beauty, you see more beauty. Gratitude for your abusive experience may come later when you realize how much you have learned and how strong you have become. It is more a feeling of gratitude for your ability to be resilient and rise above. Gratitude for your awesomeness becomes a practice in self-love!

Parenting

When our parents are not role models for good parenting, we may feel like we are flying by the seat of our pants when we have children. You may have pledged that you will never do certain things to your children that were done to you. My pledge to myself as a young mother was that I wanted my children to know how loved they are in a myriad of ways. I pledged that I would be kind. I planned on explaining to them the reasoning behind my rules. I wanted them to know that I was open to discussion when feasible.

But I made mistakes with my children that I regret. Looking back, I see that I was not aware that I had taken on some of my mother's yelling pattern. Shame storm! I so did not want to do this! My three children do not consider me to have been abusive and manipulative, but I shouted too often. I misplaced my unresolved frustration and anger about the relationship with my mother and her treatment of me, even though we lived half the world apart, sometimes onto my children. Raising children, being married, studying and working to further my career, living in a foreign country and mastering seven international moves was often stressful enough. There was not really any room in my psyche for unresolved inner conflict.

I wish that I had been farther along in healing from my abuse. I am convinced that this would have made me calmer and more playful. Then my children would have had an even better childhood. I have asked forgiveness from my children and listened to their experiences of childhood. Often parents feel some shame and embarrassment about their parenting. If there are unresolved issues and feelings of pain that your children harbor, listen to them. This will not be the time to state how you experienced their childhood. Just listen with an open heart. Maybe you can muster up a sincere apology. It will not kill you. It will not degrade you. Admission of what you did that was not so great does not negate all the good you have done by your children. What it does is let your children free themselves from their hurt.

I write this piece about parenting as a warning to do your healing work ASAP, so you do not unconsciously act out any negative family patterns with the next generation. I am convinced that deeply recovering from the after-effects of abuse, neglect and practicing good parenting ideas are the strongest safeguards to keep us all from repeating the harmful ways of behaving that we were raised with. We won't be perfect, but we will have better parenting skills.

We Came Full Circle
As I finish this chapter, it is exactly a year to the day of my mother's funeral. I visited with her for six weeks before she died. My aversion is gone, I laid my ear to her chest and listened to her heartbeat, realizing I was so close to the womb where my life began. There is such a bond between a mother and child! We spoke about death, and I admired her calm willingness to embark on a new journey. She kept telling me that she wanted me to know that she had always loved me. 'Loved but not always loving' is how I could wrap my head around her declaration. We were able to share simple love, and I will always be grateful for this time together.

My experience with my mother was my training ground for the work I do now. I trekked through the muck and struggled not to sink. Self-introspection, great studies, and meditation have pulled me out of that muck and onto a beautiful and light-filled path. Like the pearl ring that I inherited from my mom, our relationship started out as an irritation that grew into something beautiful, which is my work to help others recover from the experience of abuse.

Despite not being a perfect mom, I am proud that I broke the maternal intergenerational suppression within my family. As a result, I have respectful and loving relationships with our three wonderful children. We have very active communication and good times in our family now. I am so grateful! The beat goes on. Our children have become loving and supportive parents. It is worth noting that I've managed to stay in love and married to my husband of thirty-eight years. And I've received the greatest compliment of all; I am entrusted with the care and feeding of our beloved grandchildren.

I have learned what self-love, self-worth, and self-trust entails, and I find it crucially important to inspire others to regain their self-love.

In addition to private coaching, I've created a group course that will soon be available both locally and in cyberspace to help people bounce back from abuse faster than I did. Mothers and fathers need tools to recover from their wounding and make sure not to pass down their hurt to their children. Plans are laid to co-teach mindfulness and compassion training in schools here in Germany so children can build their resilience.

Adult children and even open-minded former abusers can learn how to repair their family relationships. I don't keep this knowledge to myself anymore. This is how I can best serve. I am living a fulfilling life, and you have it in you to do the same!

LoveRocks!
There is a place on this earth that only you can fill!

Oshikan Sjodin-Bunse

I live an intercultural lifestyle, as I have either been an expat or a re-pat since leaving Northern California in 1979. I will always be a love-pat, (those who live long-term in their partner's country) as I originally moved to Germany to be with my life partner who is now my husband of thirty-eight years. With our three children, we have moved back and forth between Germany, Japan, and the USA. My permanent residence is now Berlin.

I am a former Shiatsu therapist and teacher. This care for my fellow human beings developed into taking up studies in psychology as I became more interested in what clients told me about their lives and relationships than in giving Shiatsu treatments. I became licensed in Germany as a Heilpraktiker fuer Psychotherapie (Healing Practitioner for Psychotherapy). This training enables me to understand the psychological pathologies that may inflict us. I have also studied the other end of the spectrum; that which is right and good about us, with Martin Seligman Ph.D., and other notables in the field of The Applied Science of Positive Psychology.

I am a graduate of the Authentic Happiness Coaching program from Martin Seligman. I am a Certified Professional Coach through the International Coach Academy. I am trained in Jungian based Voice Dialogue and various forms of meditation. I will always be a student in one form or another as I have a deep love of learning.

Teleconferences, teleclasses, and coaching over the telephone have been a part of my life for sixteen years now. I began my work as a coach and facilitator by helping expats and love-pats flourish on foreign soil. I know this lifestyle well, and it was very rewarding to coach people from all over the world and present at conferences on this topic.

But alas, another deep interest of mine would call to me periodically, that of helping women and men recover from having a difficult relationship with their mothers. I was raised with emotional and verbal abuse from my mother and know the after-effects intimately of being told, through various actions and words, that, 'you're just no good.'

I've combined the lessons learned from my own recovery, compassionate care for my coaching clients, the use of researched-based exercises from positive psychology, great mind-sets and meditation techniques to create a group course for people desiring to recover from their after-effects of abuse. I also continue with my love of individual coaching.

I have heeded my inner calling and changed the focus of my business. It has become part of my deepest life fulfillment to support people in re-learning how to walk through life with a strong sense of self-love, self-worth, and self-trust after experiencing abuse. I also find it of utmost importance that parents make sure not to pass on negative family legacy patterns to their own children. I also explore with clients if and how the relationship with their mother can be salvaged.

The written word calls to me more and more, and I have had the privilege to write both a chapter detailing my story of recovery from abuse and the foreword to the second book in the series, "We Choose to Thrive."

My life is very fulfilling because it is filled with my most important values. I love to spend time with family and friends, be in nature and to coach. These beloved activities give me a great sense of life purpose and meaning.

Love Rocks!
Oshikan's Video Interview: https://youtu.be/iHn2q7Pz9JU
Website: www.loverocks.global

"Do not speak badly of yourself,
for the warrior that is inside you hears
your words and is lessened by them.
You are strong, and you are brave.
There is a nobility of spirit
within you.
Let it grow."

David Gemmell

Uncovering My Inner Truth

By Patricia Hulet

*S*ome people might say the sexual abuse I experienced wasn't extreme or I didn't have to endure great pain over long periods. Abuse is abuse, regardless of intensity. The man I truly trusted had disrespected my body at age fourteen. The fondling changed me and deeply affected my life.

The incidents caused withdrawal and loneliness, having a hard time loving myself, and hating my body. Wanting children despite the pain of intercourse, and surgeries to get rid of the endometriosis. Having an autoimmune disease because of thyroid issues and even the big C, melanoma, because an irregular mole had been metastasized by damaging sunburns and the critical thoughts I'd had about myself for years. My pain threshold became so high that I didn't take care of my body. My lack of self-care led to self-abuse and arduous suicide thoughts. Male and authority issues caused havoc not only with my father but also with my spouse and bosses.

I had learned to face the triggers and changed my beliefs, my story, and myself. I permitted to claim my own rights to have a beautiful sexual relationship. I found faith, learned to set boundaries, and experienced the miracle of giving birth after adopting two sons. I had a successful teaching and curriculum development career for 35 years. Two and a half years ago I thought I had released everything in writing and gotten to the point where the sexual abuse didn't define me anymore. I had learned to recognize the

103

old snake-skins of the past when memories or thoughts returned. They were not to make me feel ashamed, disgraced, or embarrassed. Their value was to know I was clean in that area and moving forward.

I had forgiven my father many times and knew we loved each other unconditionally, even though he never apologized. So why did the gnawing pain keep coming back? What was a root cause that wasn't yet healed? What set the stage for what happened as a teenager? Memories took me to the spankings I received as a child.

Many parents spanked their children. I knew that. part of it was I didn't understand what I had done wrong. I was just a normal, curious child. I was intelligent and needed time to process. Sometimes I didn't even remember what I had done, let alone know why it was wrong.

It took me years to grasp that I had to deal with my dad's pride and upbringing. He was a tough, farm-raised boy and kept the pain inside. His mother would ask if it hurt as she whacked a belt on his backside. He'd always answer "NO!" I tried to comprehend why he kept telling me the story. Was I supposed to hold the pain? I couldn't; I cried. Dad didn't know that disappointing him hurt me the most and then I had physical pain on top. Maybe I was too sensitive, but I always felt like he wanted to slap me longer and harder just as his mother had. And it wasn't just the spanking. Why did he have to give me a bad time for my achievements, my good grades? Was that supposed to be teasing? It didn't feel like it.

Was I also struggling with the fact that he wanted a boy and I was a girl? I knew I would never be the boy he wanted and being his only child; he would never have a son. He never stated it, but I could feel his discontent. At that young age, I took on his disappointment. No wonder I always felt like I could never please him. It's not a surprise that I was disillusioned about my role in life.

As an only child, I lived in the adult world. We did things with my parents' friends. I didn't play much with friends my own age because it caused problems. Once in fifth grade, I invited a friend home from school. My parents must have said some things to each other about having to wait up dinner. Mom told me to NEVER, ever, do it again. Though I would have gladly given up dinner just to have a friend visit, I obeyed and didn't invite anyone ever again. Even when someone came over when I was a married adult, we stood talking at the door until I finally realized I could permit myself to invite anyone I wanted to inside my own home.

Why was I left alone to my own thinking and suffering? I don't remember being hugged afterward or even comforted. Why was I never told that I was loved? I don't even remember where my mother was. It was never voiced that this was just a small thing in the long run; I could learn not to do it again, whatever it was. Not being church-goers, I was never taught that I could be forgiven. I had to deal with it on my own in silence with my little girl brain and experience. I let the survival part of my brain function shield me. I became super sensitive and aware, so I could "protect" myself.

At six years of age, over sixty years ago, I had the capacity and took on the responsibility to never be spanked again. I figured out I would punish myself before my dad could, for small infractions so I wouldn't do something bad enough to be paddled. I was forever overcritical of myself trying to be "perfect" so no one could find fault. It was easier to stay quiet, out of the way, so I didn't get into trouble. That didn't let me become friends. I was trying too hard to be what I thought I should be. People knew I was intelligent and kind, never realizing how much I tormented myself inside.

Why didn't I feel loved? I knew my parents loved me and did the best they could. So why did I sporadically get to the point where I cried uncontrollably at night, trying to be quiet. They would hear me, and we worked out some things. Why didn't I learn to talk to my parents? Why did I accept what they gave me, without anything extra? Ahhhh, it was my mother's stories of her as a little girl. When the family went to the fair, her dad might buy ice cream cones for the three girls. However, if any of them asked for one, none were purchased. Because of the number of times the story was told, I learned not to ask for anything. I did not know how to comfort or care for myself in a healthy way.

One summer when I was about twelve we were traveling in Michigan. It was pouring rain as we toured various sites. My parents were having such a wonderful time that I didn't want to spoil their fun and enjoyment of the day. So I didn't tell them my raincoat was leaking. They just noticed how soaked I was when we got to a place to dry off. "Why didn't you tell us," they asked.

Was it because I was the only child in their adult world? Fear of what my dad could do? Feeling like I could never do things right? If my own parents sometimes hurt me, who would want me? I couldn't trust myself so lost confidence.

I tried overcoming with willpower. Mind over matter is not enough. The patterns had been deeply ingrained emotionally. Willpower is defined as control and restraint. How could I exert any more control over things, especially when I was still in victim mode? I ended up containing my emotions, believing I was always unworthy.

I had promised myself I would NEVER spank my children. I was watching my hand go back and forth while inside I'm yelling STOP! I cuddled them and cried. I began reaching out to my higher self and God. Why couldn't I quit? It was hard to ask for forgiveness when I knew my hand was causing us both pain due to the anger I felt inside. I remember one time I cried for three hours after spanking my oldest. Tears flowed, and my body shook with agony as I pleaded with my Heavenly Father. I was trying to break this pattern. His peace began to enfold me, and I was given an image of old-fashioned calipers. I realized that He measured me differently than I did. He had seen my heart change, and the desire grow. It amazed me that I didn't spank my children for years after that. I had one relapse but recognized the anger I had for me was stronger than any frustration I had for what my daughter had done.

There was one time my mother was hurt by my oldest child. I sensed her anger and that she wanted me to lambaste him up one side and down the other. Instead, I gently talked to the three-year-old. Within moments, he decided he needed to apologize, so he ran off to Gramma. After that tender mercy, my mother quit instructing me what a "good mother" would do and started expressing to me what a great mother I was. Years later after a counseling session, I began to share with her what I had learned.

Invariably, her response was, "I wished I had known that sooner!"

It wasn't willpower that overcame my weaknesses. It was a firmness of mind and commitment to myself mentally and emotionally. Then as I pledged myself to a higher power, which could be personal higher self, God, or the Universe, the strength came. I noticed more "timelessness" as I carefully chose my response and became less frustrated. My desire grew stronger because I didn't give up. I was strengthened and guided to change.

Understanding grew as I read in Chapter Two of The Mastery of Love by Don Miguel Ruiz. The "Loss of Innocence" impressed me deeply (p27): *"The emotional body starts to change its tune, and it is no longer the normal tune of the human being. We play the game of the adults, we play the game of the outside Dream, and we lose. We lose our innocence, we lose our freedom, we lose our happiness, and we lose our tendency to love."*

I realized I had lost me. Understanding this encouraged me to accept and love myself more. I didn't have to apologize for others. I kept my thoughts pure by not judging, recognizing that my dad was still emotionally hurting from being, in his mind, unfairly spanked. I was running on a six-year-old nervous system. I got down to her level as her wiser adult and taught her not to waste time thinking or acting upon those old, ugly thoughts and beliefs. I began to awaken into who I AM and be my own self. It's MY LIFE, not what others think or wants me to do.

Training with Healer's Blueprint and SimplyHealedR taught me the questions I needed to ask myself to deal with the pain and heal my emotions and body. Quantum Touch refined skills. My intuition became practiced and matured. Because of what I had suffered through and survived from, I could now become a change agent. I became an advocate for:

- Forgiving ourselves and others
- Splendid-ness of being a woman
- Vitality of self-care and selfless love
- Teaching families scientific tools and skills to turn our brains and lives around
- Gratitude

- Trusting our inner truth and
- Embracing a purpose-driven life

What about my gifts and talents? What was my purpose for being here? I learned that overcoming our mess awards us with skills to edify others with a message of hope. No longer a victim, I became a champion. I could help clients release their debilitating past, choose and realign with more satisfying models of behavior and thinking patterns, rewrite and crystallize a new story of life, and emerge into their own healthy, passionate vision.

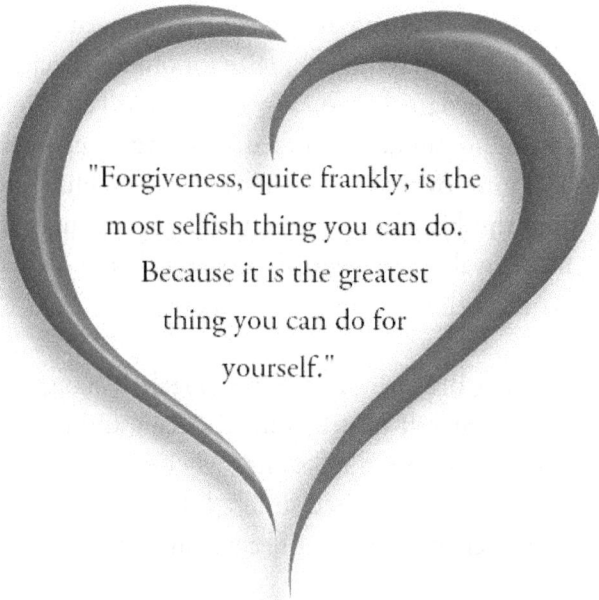

"Forgiveness, quite frankly, is the most selfish thing you can do. Because it is the greatest thing you can do for yourself."

Patricia Hulet

Patricia Hulet taught for 35 years in elementary schools where she designed curriculum. She wrote and illustrated Library Games Activity Kit, and recorded Love Your Body (Cd). She effectively instructed to a full range of learning styles using her gift to listen to the truth behind learning challenges. (She represented the state of Arizona as Teacher of the Year in an AG in the Classroom national convention). Later, she wrote for and received three separate grants to develop a Butterfly Garden for her school.

Patricia and her husband Milt live in Mesa, Arizona and have three grown children and two grandchildren. Her hobbies include weaving, tooling leather, reading, drawing, writing, traveling, being out in nature, hiking, and camping.)

Passionate about being a life-long learner, Patricia loves to teach and motivate others. She is a creative and inspiring coach, speaker, and teacher, demonstrating compassion and understanding, which gives her the innate ability to uplift and empower others to reach new heights.

Video Interview: https://youtu.be/mt0Ebcmrdyo
sunblossom@cox.net

"Forgiveness, quite frankly, is the most selfish thing you can do. Because it is the greatest thing you can do for yourself."

Get Involved in Helping Others

By Sylvia Justus

*M*y story began 68 years ago. I was born in El Paso, Texas to very young Hispanic parents. I was oldest of six children, and my childhood was dysfunctional due to alcohol abuse and infidelity. Being the oldest meant taking care and watching out for my siblings. At 17, I became pregnant and married my high school boyfriend.

This began an abusive marriage of 15 years. I once again found myself in the cycle of alcohol abuse and infidelity by my husband, along with verbal and physical abuse. I strongly believed that this situation was just part of my punishment for getting pregnant out of wedlock and deserved my pain.

When my then husband graduated from college, we moved to Boulder, Colorado. It was quite a challenge moving to a new city with a toddler, having never been away from my family and hometown. I somehow managed to survive from one day to another. I just kept thinking that if I were a better wife and mother, he would change.

A couple of years later, we had a second daughter. When she was three months old, I landed a great job with IBM and started doing well. All of the sudden my eyes and ears were open to the magical words, "good job." I thrived in my work environment and enjoyed the rewards of my

111

contributions that resulted in raises and promotions. I was very successful at work, but my home life continued to be a mess.

I was good at hiding my home life being careful to wear a smile on my face despite what I was going through. I knew that there were other women in my husband's life, but I thought I could make it till my youngest graduated from high school, but it continued to get worse.

As my daughters entered their teens, I realized that if I stayed in my abusive relationship, I would be giving them the message that it was okay to be treated badly. This realization, along with my success at my workplace somehow gave me the courage to leave my marriage when my girls were 14 & 9.

An opportunity to transfer with my team to Arizona arose, and soon I found myself as a single mom with a huge hole in my heart. I strongly believed that the "right" man in my life would fill this hole. I spent many years going from one relationship to another always searching for the "perfect" man. I was married many times over the next 15 years, and struggled with bad choices and choosing men that were more messed up than I was so I could feel okay. I lacked self-worth and truly believed I was "bad."

I continued to do well at work and moved into different management positions including a transfer to the Marketing office in Phoenix, but on the inside, I was one thread of falling apart. Always searching and seeking for something or someone better.

My healing journey finally began 20 years ago at the age of 48 when I was invited to church by my then mother-in-law to listen to her piano solo at her church. I found God that day and asked Jesus to come into my heart and be the Lord and savior of my life. I surrendered my broken heart to him, and my healing began. I began attending church and reading the bible with the help of my new church family.

Soon after this, my then husband went on a ten-day mission trip to Russia where he fell in love with his translator. Once again, I was brought down to my knees and found myself single again. The difference this time was that I had my faith, so I continued my walk with God and stood in his promises to begin to move in a new direction.

The first thing I learned was forgiveness! First, God's forgiveness of me for all of the things in my life that I felt guilty and ashamed of. Then I began to forgive my first and abusive ex-husband, my parents and those that had hurt me and those whom I had hurt along the way. I now had hope, and there was light in my life. I then learned and began the long journey of loving myself and being okay in my own skin. The hole in my heart was gone. I chose joyful hope.

During my healing, I remarried and have been married for 17 years. I retired from Corporate America after 36 years and began my own business which lasted nine years. I now finally know that everything I have been through has made me who and I am today. This journey has prepared me for my purpose in life which is to help women and girls who are going through tough situations & transitions in their lives. I plan to spend my remaining days giving back in the area of women and girls issues, such as domestic violence, teenage pregnancy/moms, single moms, divorced women, and widows.

The most positive thing I have done is to make girlfriends. During the nine years, I had my business I networked quite a bit. I forced myself to go to network events. I sold jewelry, so I went where women were. I learned and allowed myself to have fun, which was foreign to me. This helped me to slowly let others see who I was inside which I had lost along the way.

My words of wisdom that I would like to share is to get involved in helping others. I joined a wonderful organization called Soroptimist. Soroptimist is a global volunteer organization working to improve the lives of women and girls through programs leading to social and economic empowerment.

I belong to Soroptimist International of the Kachinas which has been serving the Phoenix West Valley since 1980. I am very active and currently serve as Vice-President. I love what we do to help women and girls! You can't have a pity party while you are helping others.

Additionally, I hold and lead a bible study for women going through transitions in their lives. This ministry is called "Heart 2 Heart." I continue to mentor women that are in or are leaving abusive situations.

"You are not a victim for sharing your story. You are not merely a survivor. You are now a thriver, setting the world on fire with your truth. You never know who needs your light, your warmth, your raging courage."
Alex Elle

Sylvia Justus

Suggested Resources:

Making Peace With Your Past by Tim Sledge (Help for adult children of dysfunctional families) This workbook is a 12-week study that includes reading, praying and journaling. It starts with "Discovering Self- Esteem."

"The Purpose Driven Life" by Rick Warren is another of my favorites. The book begins with the words "It's not about you" and answers the question "why am I here."

We Choose to Thrive Interview: https://youtu.be/PgquiyN2Kfs

"You gain strength, courage, and
confidence by every experience in which
you really stop to look fear in the face.
You are able to say to yourself, "I lived
through this horror. I can take the
next thing that comes along.
Eleanor Roosevelt

Forgiveness is Deciding to Let Go of the Power of Pain

By Lise Lavigne

I was a joyful and carefree little girl. I was always twirling around to music and laughing. Unfortunately, this was brought to a halt when I lost my innocence much too young. Most of the men in my family were sexual abusers or addicted to pornography. I was born in a very big family of uncles, aunts, and cousins. My parents had seven children. I was the 6th child born 12 years after my first five siblings.

At age three, the trajectory of my life changed when my older cousin abused me. He asked me to come and sit on his lap and eventually fondled me under my dress. He made me promise to keep this as our special secret otherwise it would make my aunt and uncle very sad. I was so scared and confused. Each time we visited, which was at least once a month, he would repeat his "special secret." My mother died when I was seven years old, and we didn't visit my aunts and uncles much after her death.

Sadly, other members of my family touched me very inappropriately as well. I was surrounded by sexual abusers - my uncles, other cousins, and my dad. My dad was the worst of them all when it came to abusing his children. He abused us sexually, physically and emotionally. He would beat his children with anything he could find when he got in a bad mood. I consider myself the lucky one because my sister (my only sister) developed five different personalities.

When I grew up, I was very dysfunctional in all my relationships. I married at the age of 18 because for the first time I felt loved. We were both too young to know what we were doing though. Neither of us was emotionally ready to undertake such a big commitment like marriage. I always felt empty inside and therefore looked for love outside my marriage to fill this void. After seven years I left my husband, and I proceeded onto a series of long-term and short-term relationships. I tried to find love in all the wrong places.

At about 43 years old, I had found myself once again in an unhealthy relationship, and I had had enough. The man I had been dating for over three years was a sex addict. My heart was breaking, and I didn't know what to do. All I knew was that my life had to be different. I wanted another kind of life. The pain was so unbearable that I just wanted to die. I then fell on my knees and cried out to God and said, "God, I don't want this life anymore. Please help me."

Suddenly, there was a peace that came over me like a knowing that everything was going to be okay. Within days of praying, I came across a television program, and the lady was talking about being sexually abused by her father. I could relate to everything she was saying. I had never heard this subject talked about before. It opened up my eyes, and I felt hopeful for my life.

Eventually, I started attending a church, and they were offering a 9-month program called Freedom Session. I joined that program to discover the reason why I was attracting the kinds of relationships I found myself in continually. I had no idea that the feelings I had and the actions I chose as an adult were because of being sexually abused. The abuse was not on my mind on a regular basis. I rarely thought about it, but of course, the effects are there in our heart and our subconscious.

All my life, I had considered myself unworthy. My self-esteem was so very low. I felt a lot of shame and brokenness. I found my value in sex because that's the only thing I knew. To get attention I had to have sex. If I didn't get sex, then I didn't get love. I was a great seducer of men, and I had many boyfriends. I was living in pain and, most of the time, I didn't realize it because I was numbing it so well with men, romance, shopping, and working.

When I became aware that I have value, my standards rose up. My value doesn't come from sex. I've learned how to love myself and accept the events that occurred between the ages of 3 to 12. Yes, that was my lot in life. It was what I had experienced, but I didn't have to live with the pain of the past. I didn't have to let it affect me. I learned to love myself and appreciate who I truly am. I learned that I am valuable.

It was a true eye-opener for me. It didn't mean that I had to be unhappy forever. I learned how to be happy on my own. I can be happy, and I can truly love myself. I never knew that happiness and love is an inside job. I am living and thriving now. To think that I tried to kill myself three times in the past! Life is so very precious and worth living. I was trying to get love from everybody else and everything else. I took my power back and started to love myself for the very first time.

When we want something to change and are seeking how to do that, God helps us find a way. I started to pray regularly and meditate as well. I was so hungry to make a difference in my life that I was spending 4 to 6 hours a day reading books and watching self-development and motivational videos. I also attended seminars and workshops. If you want to start the healing, I recommend the following two books: The Courage to Heal and Heal Your Life.

After my healing, there came a time when I seriously wanted to dedicate my life helping other women, so I wrote my book called "Enough is Enough."

I became a certified life coach and created coaching programs for women. I am now a motivational speaker and want to share my story worldwide to make an impact in this world. I tell my story with as many people as possible through various means such as talks, workshops, books, social media, coaching and so one.

Most of us keep these secrets inside, and we dare not tell our story to anyone because it's too shameful. It was by sharing my own story back in 2010 that my life started to heal and transform. We can't just keep it in. It will fester inside and hurt us. Find the strength to tell one person. You are not alone. Believe me; your secret is similar to other secrets.

We must accept the events that happened and believe that we can change our lives. Letting go of the pain was a big transformation for me. I forgave my dad, the uncles, the cousins. Forgiveness does not mean it was okay for them to behave that way and that everything will be back to normal. Forgiveness is deciding to let go of the power that this pain has over us and deciding to take our power back!

Keep releasing the pain and the secrets inside. Be brave and courageous. Find one person you can trust and tell them your story. Let the healing begin.

Lise Lavigne

Lise Lavigne disrupts the status quo in women's lives so they can break free from emotional pain and flood the world with love. She is an empowerment coach, bestselling author and motivational speaker. Her passion is seeing the powerful transformation women make in their lives once they let go of their abusive past. She inspires and teaches women how to find peace, acceptance and self-love.

She is also the author of "Enough is Enough!," and the bestselling book WOW Woman of Worth - Looking for Love in All the Wrong Places. With her skills, love and compassion, Lise helps women attract healthy relationships by first taking their power back.

Website: www.liselavigne.com
Instagram : liselavigne_coaching
Facebook page: Lise Lavigne Coaching
For my Free Course: http://liselavigne.com/take-power-back/
Video interview: https://youtu.be/7BEzh3FF-RQ

"Forgiveness, quite frankly, is the
most selfish thing you can do.
Because it is the greatest
thing you can do for
yourself."

Awesomeness Starts With You!

By Julianna Rivera

*L*aughing at myself sitting in a neighbor's dark cold garage covered in bed bug bites, itch cream on a duck taped mattress listening to free personal development audio off SoundCloud; I knew I had changed! There are definitely those personal ah-ha moments that happen for a reason! Mine were barely starting and at twenty-two years old! My heart and mind synonymously put the following events into mini titled snapshots. I am nowhere near perfect as a human being. This is purely to share and continue to learn that one's past does not determine their future! By no means do I mean to put anyone down or anyone's present personal experiences aside, as "Comparison is the Thief of Joy."

I knew I was living in a negative toxic living environment that I had wanted out of for some time. Home was not home to me. When I was very young my dad had very erratic behavior. He would yell and scream for no reason. The one time I tried asking for help with homework, he ended up screaming and created more destruction by breaking my pencils. He often threw things when he was mad. His anger was scary, as once he almost broke his steering wheel off of his truck. Often going to the extreme to prove a point, he once threatened me with a paperweight to crush my fingers. He went into rages that affected everyone.

123

Looking back this all seems so crazy to me, to have to live like that. He would often bring presents to try and smooth over his past behavior.

It was around this time when my mom and dad divorced which was beyond difficult and devastating for me. Having to ping pong each week back and forth to my mom and dad's house wasn't easy, never knowing what type of mood or experience I'd leave with. This went on for more than three years. I remember when I was a teenager, my mom and sister had a rough knock down, drag out fight that my dad luckily was able to break up before the police were called.

Over the course of a five year period, after my dad passed away, came even more severe manipulation and abuse from my mom and sister. Each of us was on completely different life paths, all wanting different things. We each had our own past and present demons we carried within, that I saw turn them into people I no longer recognized. I couldn't ignore the negative way in which they lived and how they treated me. There parental ways and values were very backwards.

My sister had many toxic relationships and both my mom and sister had unpredictable daily personality shifts. There was constant stress about petty things on a daily basis that I was absolutely done with. Having to question and tip-toe on every thought you had wasn't a way to live. I was betrayed by them as my family, and had proof that I had been taken advantage of financially. I sought out second opinions from different people both professional and personal, that I trusted more than my own family.

There was no aura of love and support going on. I had emotional chaos inside and suppressed pain that I didn't know what to do with, from the years of mental abuse as a young adult and child. Anytime I was home with my mom and sister, I could always feel bitterness and resentment in the air. Almost as if we were all just unpleasant roommates forced to live together and be around each other. I never wanted to be home. I would rather work two jobs and spend my spare time at the gym with a friend. I would pack a lunch box from the groceries I had to buy for myself and keep them in my car just so I wouldn't have to stop at home to eat.

I got creative with figuring out what dry foods that wouldn't go bad. I would pack everything I needed for the day, as well as anything that I was worried they might eat or use up while I was gone. I became an expert at having to hide toiletries and dry goods in my room, so they wouldn't take them, as there was no lock on my door. I would always take my toiletries into the bathroom to shower and then take them back into my room and have to hide them again.

Life there was your on your own, with no support, love or guidance. There were no boundaries or respect for anyone else's things. My mom would use verbal threats quite often to get her way with money. She would threaten not to take me to work unless I gave her money to pay her bills. My sister would often make me wait hours to pick me up from work. She would show up and take me home only if I had the exact amount of gas money she wanted just for that drive home. I often had to wait long hours after working long shifts to get a ride. Everything was a game.

I looked forward to the day when I would have some freedom and not have to deal with all the negotiations to get to and from work. I was working two different jobs in an effort to save for a car, but that was never an option with having to get all my groceries, toilet paper, gas, insurance etc. When they did show up, I was forced to listen to arguing the ride home and had to pay both of them money for gas for their cars. I would often have to pay for Uber or Lyft because no one would show up. I was tired of wasting my days just for rides home. I was never able to properly save up money.

To their advantage, they forced a sour car deal in my lap to take over. I was the second person they tried to pawn the car off on. The whole thing was a ridiculous ordeal. Neither wanted to be held accountable. My sister didn't care, she set out and got into a new car for herself. The old car was in my mom's name as my sister's co-signer. She did not want to take full responsibility for what they had done, before or after I took over the payments.

I clearly remember the day they picked me up from work actually on time and for once in a pleasant manner. They took me to my bank without asking to pull out $500 cash to pay the deductible for my sister's car who

125

she lent to a pregnant friend, who got it into a car accident without a license and mysteriously went missing and stop paying the car payments. My mom and sister once again came up with a plan and manipulated the situation. I was told there would be no more rides, and I had to take over the payments. I was informed by a close friend who worked at a bank, that the entire thing was preposterous and being so young it was financial suicide to take on such a high risk.

I was betrayed by my family, had proof of it, and knew I was being taken advantage of financially. I sought out second opinions from different people I trusted more. Such opinions were both professional and personal. After getting different opinions about my car situation, I realized I was being royally screwed! This made me furious. I wasn't building my own credit and had no payment history to show for this. I carried more internal stress knowing what my mom and sister were doing to me. They only cared that the payments were being made and that it wasn't coming out of there pockets. Each time I confided in a close friend, their sincere concern only confirmed my stress about this car situation.

Being kept in the dark regarding such matters only made me not trust them even more. My mom would often threaten if I wanted A/C in the Arizona summertime, I would have to pay half the bill. They were constantly either bribing me, guilting me or tricking me out of my hard earned money. At this time, I had reached my last straw and had come to the realization that my sister's personality had truly changed. She was unrecognizable to me as a person and as a sister.

The best way I can describe what happened to me next is that a greater force than myself wanted to get me out of that living situation to be turned on my own new leaf! I call it "The Blow Up" when everything hit the fan. The domestic violence altercation I experienced happened May 5th, 2017. I did not start the argument and fight or initiate it. Things escalated very quickly as my sister was relentless. I remember being hit in the face repeatedly then being held down and beat up on the kitchen floor. I tried to get up and protect myself. My mom tried getting in the middle of everything and then joined in with my sister.

Now I was being attacked by two. I was thrown out of the front door onto a ladder standing up against a tree close by in the front yard. I was forced outside the outer gate, and no longer had my shoes on. Everything happened so fast; I didn't realize how much blood was on my face and running in my black eye. I was in shock and full of adrenaline from what had just happened. I was left with blood all over, bruises on face, my shirt torn off, thankfully my bra still intact, no shoes, one earring, body bruises, and un-glamorous pictures for proof. A random person driving by witnessed everything. Showing concern the lady asked me if I wanted her to call the cops.

My mom and sister paused, realizing that they would be in trouble if the cops saw the messed up shape I was in. Then, they yelled at the lady to go away, and call the cops on me and not them. I knew they had figured out a way to cover up what they had done to me. They did not allow me to get my cell phone, or car keys, that was on my bed back inside the house. The kind lady thankfully drove back around to find me walking in my neighborhood looking like I did. I was grateful to be able to go nearby to a good friend and neighbor I trusted.

I had no idea how bad I looked until he told me to go inside and look at my face in the mirror, I was beyond horrified. My face was swollen. I made the decision to call the cops to protect myself, as I thought my face alone would be proof enough of what they had done to me. I was wrong. When the cops showed up, they didn't ask me any questions and just put me in cuffs. The neighbor and I were in disbelief as to why.

Out of the cop car I could see two cops talking to my mom and sister for what seemed like forever. I felt I didn't get to voice my side of what had happened. I saw my mom pat the cop on the shoulder trying to lighten the situation. The amount of time they had spoken to my mom and sister about what happened was nowhere near the time they gave me to try and explain. I was mystified as to how this was all turning out.

Sitting twisted in the cop car with the metal cuffs hurting my wrists, I saw my mom out the window sweeping leaves on her front sidewalk like it was a normal day. When the cop came back over to me and opened the car door to ask me something, I pointed out my mom and her abnormal behavior on the other side of the street. I couldn't believe she was sweeping like strawberry shortcake while her youngest daughter was sitting bleeding in the back of a cop car. I still don't understand the reasoning the cops gave to as why I was the one that was to be held accountable.

Each time a close friend or family member has asked me what happened, they too show their astonishment as to why I was the one arrested. I had no choice and was forced to spend the night in jail. I was arrested although I had no history of violence whatsoever. I was promised no felony charge. My record had been clean.

My mom and I were supposed to fly out to California the morning of May 6th for my grandma's 84th birthday celebration. I was beyond sad and upset I missed that. I t hurt me and tore me apart even while sitting in jail. I felt terrible and was crying over it for some time. I knew my mom went on the trip regardless of the new fact that her youngest daughter was wrongly jailed. The next 24 hours were the longest moments of my life. After being released I had no place to go but knew I had little time to figure out my next moves for my safety and survival.

Saying this was a turning point is an understatement! I found out who was really there for me in every way and I gained MAJOR PERSPECTIVE very quickly. I was forced to mature quicker now that I was completely without a family and out on my own. I had always imagined the day I would get to move out, but it was never like this. I now had to match my desire to change along with the better life I imagined for myself. I often turned to Personal Development.

I was always willing to work hard but I found my biggest obstacle preventing me was the negative atmosphere I was once in. I had to make some major decisions quickly and create some clear goals immediately. I saw myself jumping into real productive actions. I found some traits in myself that surprised me. I realized when I put my mind to something, I can do anything.

In the next months that followed I spent much time getting my new life in order and breaking free from my old family. I was healing slowly, both mentally and physically. My next steps formed into crystal clear action steps. Two words that stayed with me the entire time from previous personal development were "FAIL FORWARD!" There is no true learning without mistakes. I was on my own and had to stick it out, do it for myself as no one was going to pick me up but me! Through my own self-growth no matter how difficult a situation became I kept the same supportive friends and mindset around me.

The saying "Pressure Makes Diamonds" became very familiar as I had never experienced maturity so fast before. It pushed me to adult quickly and think, act, behave and get things done for myself. I was utilizing resources and discovered new capabilities within myself I never knew existed.

Even though things were moving forward, I was exhausted, stressed out and had to remain healthy because I could not afford to take a day off from work. One major bump in the road that I experienced, was when I was offered an inexpensive safe house to live, in a bad part of town. Not having my father there was truly difficult when I found I wish I could reach out to him about all of what happened.

Even though my father and I had a broken relationship, I missed him after he passed away. It felt he was a missing puzzle piece in this journey to create a better me and life. After staying in this shelter for less than a week, I ended up in Urgent Care, my skin in massive shock from being covered in bed bug bites head to toe. I was told I'd have to be given a large dose of steroids as my skin was hot and puffy. It was so scary almost passing out face first on the floor from the dosage. I have never been in so much discomfort. I had to hide it as much as I could at work. It took my body weeks to recover from my skin feeling like it was on fire and itching. Sanitizing and getting rid of all the bugs felt like it took forever to ensure I did not take the bugs with me. I ended up finding a much better place to live - bedbug-free!

I managed to get some belongings out of my mom's house. I had to call and arrange a police escort. You were only allowed 15 minutes of protection to get in and out with whatever you could. It was a mad scramble to get the important documents and items I needed. I spent the next couple weeks getting a new bank account that couldn't get hacked into, my own personal P.O. Box and separated my payment and phone plan. In all of this, I found my mom also scammed the government and claimed me as an independent to try and get the money that was rightfully mine as I was the one busting my butt working two jobs while she was unemployed during that time. Once again, another way my family kept me from moving forward financially. As a young adult, you would think your parent would want to give you guidance to become responsible! Not mine!

What I have learned is, no matter where you are in life, what you choose to do with your time can make a big difference in success or failure. Time doesn't wait for you to get your act together. You can choose daily productive choices to move towards a better life, or choose the easy way and stay where you are. Even through those activities might be small and easy to do, they are also easy not to do, especially after working two jobs.

What I have learned through my personal development is those positive everyday activities accumulate over time, taking you one step closer to your goals to a better life. I had to learn to roll with things as they came. Rolling with the punches, learning, making mistakes and trying again. I learned to look for the lessons and see EVERYTHING as a guidepost, possibly wrapped in fear and negativity at first.

Through building my new fresh start however ugly and rough it seemed, I had to face my fears and emotions that came with that one step at a time. Each day I had to almost look outside myself and compare back to where I was, making sure I wasn't moving backward with my personal growth. I had to force myself to be conscious and aware of every decision I made, and where to spend every ounce of energy.

I now got to choose the people I wanted to keep in my life and surround myself with their love and support from here on out. Even though I had lost my real family, I chose to see it as I had gained a new type of love and family all around me. All of these changes continue to affect me in a much more positive and healthy way. This was a major reflection time and learning curve. I slowly began getting used to the new positive idea of living for me! Living in the now and present moment, with my new "Life Pillars" and lessons learned which continue to make a stronger foundation moving forward.

The remarkable clear NEW SELF AWARENESS has helped me to see what I don't want in my life, and it helps to keep me focused. Seeing the importance of one's inner circle at any age is universal. You become and mirror who you are around most. It can be positive or negative depending on who you choose to surround yourself with.

First, love yourself, develop and do you! Take the time to think about what you truly want in life, in every area and set steps to achieve them. Invest in personal development! The power of discipline in action, inner self-talk, mindset, goals and consistency are truly your secret sauce! I have noticed I am happier in my new living environment. I found myself waiting hours in line at the DES to see if I qualified for grocery assistance and health insurance, but I felt proud as I was now supporting myself.

I am grateful for what I have now. I never really understood what it meant when people always said: "Don't go through life with blinders on." That speaks volume in different ways to me now, as does everything. Blinders can be how your family chooses to live with their bad habits, personalities and certain traits that don't make you want to come around. Blinders can be the very thing that one may keep on as a protection mechanism or a form of self-doubt.

What happened to me was a blessing in disguise, the best worse thing that could have ever happened to me. Sometimes you have to do it hard, to get it done. I have no idea how I would have been able to break free of my toxic living situation, if everything hadn't happened like it did. I was in a negative headspace and felt trapped. There was definitely negativity renting space in my mind. I knew I wanted that to change, and it had to start with me. It gave me the opportunity to grow as a individual and see what I am really made out of.

At first, I would have random painful visual memories throughout my day.

Slowly as time had passed, those visions have turned into new vibrant life goals, new dreams, new healthy friends and family I care for, and choose to be around. Stronger priorities and wisdom filled those gaps little by little.

The anger slowly lessened each time when I heard, saw or mentioned my past. Today, I thrive by taking time for myself, journaling, incorporating personal development and dream boards. Spending quality time with real friends and there support has made my healing journey that much more bearable. For me, healthy advice hurt at first, it has to be taken with a grain of salt and taken right to the heart! What you may not want to hear and accept, may very well be what you need to work on or face.

The main wounds that stand out for me are; divorce, mental and emotional abuse from youth, a broken and missing father-daughter relationship, unhealthy closure through the passing of my father, being born into a family that I could no longer be apart of, no other in-state family support, unresolved anger from my youth, and not having a voice. There isn't a test or a recipe for healing. This realization caused me to not be hard on myself. There is no wrong or right way to heal, it's your journey, make it so! Allow yourself the freedom to create your new you and daily disciplines and mantras for you, to you and by you!!

I encourage and implore young adults to speak up more and reach out in healthy ways to heal any type of trauma from there past, don't wait! Such lessons will come along the way: overcoming self-hindrance, taking massive action, and seeing that holding onto pain and anger is detrimental. I found that putting positive energy about your personal goals into the universe matters! I strongly feel it's never too late to work on your most important project: YOU!! Embrace the struggle, as strength grows from it.

My biggest takeaway, believe in yourself first, always and forever!

Awesomeness starts with you!
To a better you and badass self!
Much love and growth,

Julianna Rivera

Julianna Rivera

Julianna is a natural people person with a energetic spirit! She welcomes challenges that help her be comfortable with being uncomfortable! She seeks positive opportunities to grow through motivation and to crush her goals! Keeping an open mind has definitely paid off. She's a passionate, hard working leader welcoming ways to build new wisdom.

Currently she resides and works in Arizona. Her passion for helping others and looking at the bigger picture continues to grow! She looks forward to the day when she'll be traveling, speaking and providing the strength from lessons she's learned bilingually to people from all over. Everyone should have the guidance of personal development. Helping others define there value and really visualize a better them is a journey she has willingly embarked upon.

For Julianna, everything is a learning experience.

To growth and learning!

Julianna's Interview: https://youtu.be/aSnQO_rfYyk

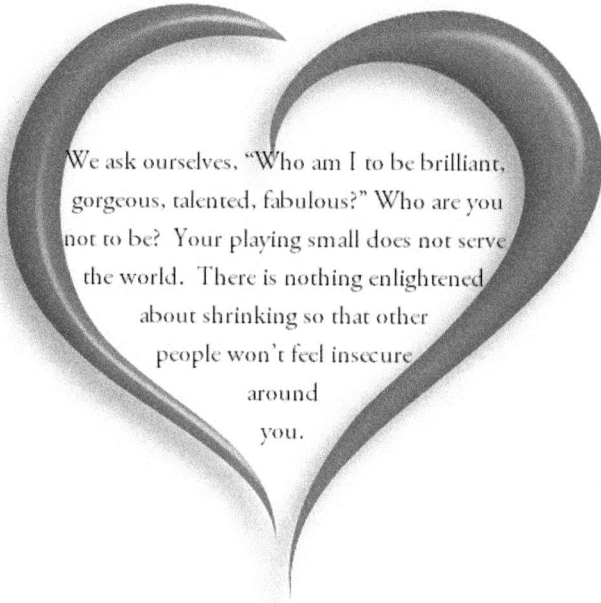

We ask ourselves, "Who am I to be brilliant,
gorgeous, talented, fabulous?" Who are you
not to be? Your playing small does not serve
the world. There is nothing enlightened
about shrinking so that other
people won't feel insecure
around
you.

Conclusion

*A*s we conclude book 2 of our We Choose to Thrive series, each of us wish to send our collective heartfelt love and support to you.

We hope our stories made an impact on you. Each of the co-authors in this book have shared their contact information. If someone resonates with you, reach out to them.

The bottom line is that it is your time to shine. If you need support in any way, or are currently enduring abuse, please seek help. Do not try to bear this alone.

Our next chapter lists resources that are available, but bottom line, the majority of communities have resources availble. Seek them out. Sadly, this is a universal issue, and many are filled with passion and a heart to help.

Love yourself enough to rise above this and live. Truly live!

To you. To Life. To a life well lived! To the decision to heal.

Choose to Thrive!

Potatoes, Eggs, or Coffee

(original source unknown)

A young woman went to her mother and told her about her life and how things were so hard for her. She did not know how she was going to make it and wanted to give up She was tired of fighting and struggling. It seemed as one problem was solved, a new one arose.

Her mother took her to the kitchen. She filled three pots with water and placed each on a high fire. Soon the pots came to boil.

- In the first she placed carrots.
- In the second she placed eggs
- In the last she placed ground coffee beans.

She let them sit and boil; without saying a word.

In about twenty minutes she turned off the burners.

- She fished the potatoes out and placed them in a bowl.
- She pulled the eggs out and placed them in a bowl.
- She ladled the coffee out and placed it in a bowl.

Turning to her daughter, she asked, "Tell me what you see."

"Potatoes, eggs, and coffee," she replied.

Her mother brought her closer and asked her to feel the potatoes. She did and noted that they were soft. The mother then asked the daughter to take an egg and break it. After pulling off the shell, she observed the hard-boiled egg.

Finally, the mother asked the daughter to sip the coffee. The daughter smiled, as she tasted its rich aroma the daughter then asked, "What are you trying to say, mother?"

Her mother explained that each of these objects had faced the same adversity: boiling water. Yet each reacted differently.

The potato went in strong, hard, and unrelenting. However, after being subjected to the boiling water, it softened and became weak.

The egg had been fragile. Its thin outer shell had protected its liquid interior, but after sitting through the boiling water, its insides became hardened.

The coffee beans were unique, however. After they were in the boiling water, they had changed the water!

And then she asked her daughter....

"When adversity knocks on your door, how do you respond? Are you a potato, an egg, or a coffee bean?

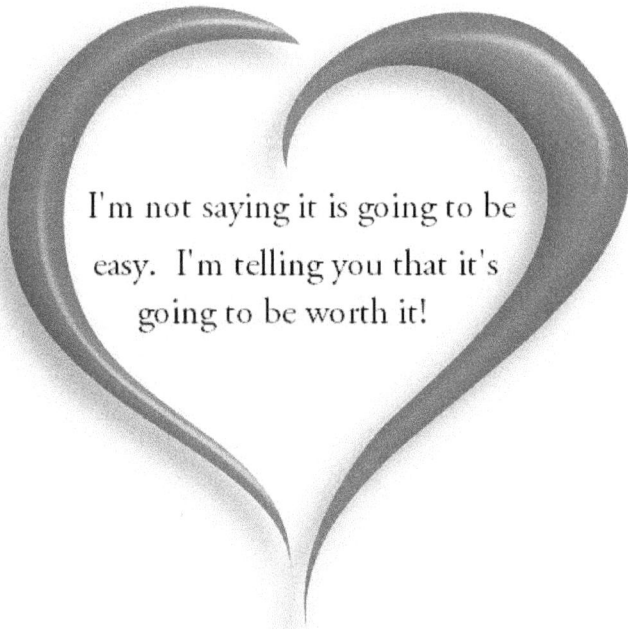

I'm not saying it is going to be easy. I'm telling you that it's going to be worth it!

www.ingramcontent.com/pod-product-compliance
Lightning Source LLC
Chambersburg PA
CBHW052008090426
42741CB00008B/1602